D1045520

"I share Scott Wilkins's passion for evangelism. The stra[...]
relationship building is a great one. I hope that REAC[...]
tionship at a time. God bless our shared vision to reach the world for Christ."

Rick Warren, senior pastor, Saddleback Church, Lake Forest, California

"A must-read for those looking for a new lease on evangelistic effectiveness. Dr. Wilkins's REACH Team ministry demonstrates the powerful effect of wedding Great Commandment acts of kindness with Great Commission witness training in a team approach that incorporates the unique gifts and abilities of every member. As a pastor and trainer of evangelists for nearly thirty years, I highly recommend Dr. Wilkins's practical steps and keen insights for taking your evangelism ministry to the next level."

Ken Silva, Evangelism Explosion International, U.S. director, western states

"Scott Wilkins writes plainly about his passion: reaching people! A simple, understandable approach, *REACH* will help those who are tired of seeing evangelism as a program and want to see it as a relationship with people."

Leighton Ford, president, Leighton Ford Ministries, Charlotte, North Carolina

"Scott Wilkins is a practitioner. He has implemented the REACH strategy in his local church setting. It works! Regardless of the approach a church uses to equip believers to witness, REACH is a relationally focused deployment strategy that engages witnesses in the lives of the unsaved. REACH is doable in virtually any size or style congregation in almost any location. *REACH* is a worthwhile tool for the toolbox of any twenty-first-century congregation interested in engaging the culture and reaching the unsaved with the gospel."

John O. Yarbrough, vice president, evangelization,
North American Mission Board, Southern Baptist Convention

"*REACH* is a timely, needed book that will do more to help us to fulfill the Great Commission than any book I've read in recent years. I believe in relational evangelism and acts of hospitality as important elements toward New Testament evangelism. Every evangelical church needs to consider putting these timely and imperative principles into practice."

Dale Galloway, dean of Beeson Institute at Asbury Seminary, Wilmore, Kentucky

"Scott Wilkins has written a vital, provocative, and innovative book dealing with bringing souls to Jesus Christ. I am excited and happy for this work and trust that it will be a blessing to many."

Adrian Rogers, senior pastor, Bellevue Baptist Church, Memphis, Tennessee

"If we do not determine to do evangelism in a more compelling way, we will lose America. Evangelism is about relationships and earning the right with your community to share Christ. In Scott Wilkins's new book, *REACH*, he has provided a strategy for Christians to embrace worldwide that will open doors into the hearts of the unchurched and the hearts of our post-Christian culture. This book will not only equip you with thoughts about what we should do, but provide you ways to do it! Implement the heart of this book and your unchurched world will become smaller."

Ronnie Floyd, pastor, First Baptist Church, Springdale, Arkansas

"Significant! *REACH* has been birthed out of a great sense of need in the evangelical church. Scott Wilkins has written the new standard in evangelism for the outreach-minded church. This book is jammed full with practical helps on how to do evangelism in the local church. It is realistic. It is easy to follow. Most importantly, it is something every church can do with committed laypeople. Full of how-tos and why-tos, all that is missing is the want to. Add that and watch your church grow. This is a must-read for pastors and churches desiring to lead their community to Christ. Both pastor and laity alike will find this a great resource. I love this book because Scott loves lost people and wants to communicate an excellent way to train up your church to reach the lost in North America. *REACH* is loaded with practical yet profound insights. This work forces us to rethink how we approach evangelism in the local church and gives us both practical and evangelistic methodologies for achieving victory. Evangelism is attainable."

Tom Cheyney, manager, strategic resourcing, Church Planting Group,
North American Mission Board, Southern Baptist Convention

"Since I personally know the author, I was excited to read his interest in evangelism. The written page matches his lifestyle as a winner of souls. This is the freshest approach to evangelism in years and could be a giant step toward genuine revival."

Bailey E. Smith, Bailey Smith Ministries, Atlanta, Georgia

"*REACH: A Team Approach to Evangelism and Assimilation* by Scott Wilkins is an excellent, practical work that will effectively enhance personal evangelism through local churches. It can be a great component to empower a church's total evangelism strategy. It will help pastors and church leaders involve their people in utilizing a 'can do' in reaching the lost and unchurched. Scott is not a theorist but has modeled *REACH* in his church. It gives the how-to for believers individually and in *teamship* to develop relationships, cultivate through acts of hospitality, lead people to Christ and help assimilate them into the life of the church. I have carefully read the material and pray that every church will implement this good approach for reaching people and bringing glory to our Lord."

Darrell W. Robinson, president, Total Church Life Ministries

"Finally, an easy to understand model for strategic planning that will fit any congregation. *REACH* is biblically based and evangelistically driven with the ultimate goal of impacting the unsaved world. Most importantly, Dr. Wilkins didn't formulate *REACH* in a classroom far away from the daily challenges of genuine ministry. On the contrary, *REACH* grew out of real-world experiences and frustrations combined with a pastor's heartfelt desire to reach his community for Christ. I am impressed with the results! Check it out!"

David Wheeler, evangelism resource group leader, State Convention of Baptists in Ohio

"Looking for something that works in personal evangelism? REACH is that process for which you are looking. The concepts of REACH are tried and proven in reaching the people in our society. This process is incarnational and biblical. You will be glad that you implemented REACH."

Malcolm McDow, professor of evangelism, George W. Truett Chair of Ministry,
Southwestern Baptist Theological Seminary

"Has your church grown weary in its feel for the Great Commission? Scott Wilkins equips us to impact the kingdom of God through the winning of souls with a practical and effective team approach. Let's REACH the lost for Christ. Evangelism doesn't have to be hard."

Bob Russell, senior pastor, Southeast Christian Church, Louisville, Kentucky

"*REACH* is a simple yet profound approach to reaching people for Christ. There is no shortage of approaches in the church that have attempted to bring our friends and neighbors to Christ, but frankly, most of them are just too complicated and scary for the average person to relate to. Scott Wilkins has done the body of Christ a big favor in putting this handy book together. It's the best thinking on evangelism that I have seen in some time. I highly recommend this work!"

Steve Sjogren, author, *Irresistible Evangelism*

"No excuses! Here is a track your church can run on. Biblical, practical, and completely fulfilling the Great Commission. *REACH* is a detailed roadmap to help do the Great Commission. We must keep fishing until the nets are full, and the methods conveyed in this book will help us to accomplish our task."

William Fay, evangelist; author, *Share Jesus Without Fear*

"Scott Wilkins has done the church of the Lord Jesus Christ a tremendous service by writing this book on evangelism. There must be a twenty-first-century strategy for reaching twenty-first-century unchurched people. In this book, a strategy that will be tremendously effective has been laid out. This book pulsates with the heartbeat of a man who wants to enable the church to be as effective as it can in carrying out the Great Commission. In my opinion, Scott has succeeded beyond perhaps his own wildest imagination."

James Merritt, pastor, Cross Pointe—the Church at Gwinnett Center, Duluth, Georgia

"Scott Wilkins draws upon his successful experiences and the best research available to develop a relational team approach to evangelism, anchored in the Bible, that works in a postmodern world. The approach reduces barriers to participation by developing natural contacts and relationships into bridges for the gospel and connections for assimilation. The team approach provides encouragement and support that inspire ongoing ministry and evangelism. The book is filled with practical helps with cultivation, hospitality, sharing your story, one verse witnessing, answering questions, interactive student guide, and much more. REACH Team is the best approach that I have seen that is intentional, relational, and practical. It will be a powerful tool for church leaders to use in equipping laypersons in relational evangelism."

Bill F. Mackey, executive director, Kentucky Baptist Convention

"Scott Wilkins is a committed pastor with a true vision for evangelism and the ability to mobilize laypersons to reach persons for Christ and then bring them into the full life of the church. We should celebrate the publication of this new book and hope that it gets in the hands of every evangelical pastor."

R. Albert Mohler Jr., president, Southern Baptist Theological Seminary, Louisville, Kentucky

"REACH: A Team Approach to Evangelism and Assimilation is a clear, concise, and practical strategy for New Testament evangelization in the twenty-first-century unchurched generation. This is a must read for pastors and churches who are truly committed to church growth and reaching the harvest. Read it, use it, and grow!"

Jerry Falwell, founder and chancellor, Liberty University, Lynchburg, Virginia

"I am always excited to find new books that will help the local church and its members fulfill the Great Commission. REACH is not a theoretical book but a practical one. This book will provide a strategic plan that will enable everyone to get involved in the most exciting project on the planet—extending the kingdom through our personal witness. Scott gives us practical suggestions that are believable, doable, and applicable. The foundation is solidly biblical, and the method is refreshingly relational. He provides suggestions for a variety of materials that will help you feel comfortable sharing your faith in the marketplace."

Ken Hemphill, national strategist, Empowering Kingdom Growth; former president, Southwestern Baptist Theological Seminary

"Scott Wilkins has provided a great service to the church by outlining an exciting strategy of evangelizing people in our modern culture. The implications of this work move us one step closer to impacting the ever-increasing mission field of North America. This work forces us to rethink how we approach our evangelism strategy and gives us both practical and missional insights to achieve. I recommend this book as required reading for pastors and laypeople throughout all evangelical churches."

John Ed Matheson, pastor, Frazer United Methodist Church, Montgomery, Alabama

"No one knows the depths of the ministry like Scott Wilkins. Do not simply read this book; devour it. His wisdom is not only profound, it is practical was well. You will be glad you did."

Ergun Mehmet Caner, professor of systematic theology and church history, Liberty University, Lynchburg, Virginia

REACH

REACH

A *TEAM* APPROACH TO EVANGELISM AND ASSIMILATION

SCOTT G. WILKINS

BakerBooks

Grand Rapids, Michigan

© 2005 by Scott G. Wilkins

Published by Baker Books
a division of Baker Publishing Group
P.O. Box 6287, Grand Rapids, MI 49516-6287
www.bakerbooks.com

Printed in the United States of America

Library of Congress Cataloging-in-Publication Data
Wilkins, Scott G., 1961–
    Reach : a team approach to evangelism and assimilation / Scott G. Wilkins.
        p.   cm.
    Includes bibliographical references (p.   ).
    ISBN 0-8010-6509-7 (pbk.)
    1. Evangelistic work. 2. Christianity and culture. 3. Acculturation 4. Assimilation (Sociology) I. Title.
BV3793.W478   2005
269′.2—dc22   2004020402

To my former, faithful church family at Fall Creek Baptist Church, Indianapolis, Indiana: Thanks for embodying God's love, grace, and encouragement, and for your willingness to allow me to dream as a pastor.

To the ever-growing and expanding Master's Church, Lexington, Kentucky: Thanks for buying in to this dream and expanding it beyond my limited vision. Your support is forever appreciated.

And to my wife, Patty: Thanks for your patience, support, and encouragement along the way. By God's amazing grace, we have journeyed this path together with great joy and reward.

Contents

PART 3
UNDERSTANDING THE STRATEGY
OF REACH TEAM

Acknowledgments

Special thanks goes to:

Dr. Malcom McDow. The genesis of this project began as a result of your transparent teaching and zeal for evangelizing our lost world. Thank you for birthing in me a similar desire to see people come to faith in Jesus Christ.

Dr. John Yarbrough and the great staff who comprise the evangelism department for the North American Mission Board of the Southern Baptist Convention. Thank you for the dialogue, ideas, and support in making *REACH* become a reality.

Dr. Darrell Robinson. Thanks for your insights, wisdom, and constructive critique. I am forever grateful.

The great people at Baker Publishing Group. Thanks to Vicki Crumpton for the initial investment of time and trust concerning the development of this work. Thanks also to Kelley Meyne for the editorial advice and instruction offered along the way. It's been a delightful experience to work with you all.

Introduction

What Is REACH Team?

Why another book on evangelism? Let's face it, the Christian market is flooded with books, conferences, seminars, and video series on church evangelism. Pastors' libraries are loaded with books on how to win the unchurched to faith in Jesus Christ. Perhaps you are also thinking, *Why do we need another approach to evangelism when we already have plenty of working models in the church?* A good question. There are more churches than ever before. Parachurch ministries are flourishing. More Christian resources are offered to the church than could ever be read, viewed, or applied. Megachurches are springing up all across America, Asia, Africa, and South America. Unique, relevant, and creative methods of communicating the gospel message develop at a whirlwind pace. So why another book on church evangelism?

What you hold in your hand will challenge you to rethink evangelism in the local church. Granted, what you are about to read is by no means "new revelation" or mystical, magical formulas to promote instantaneous growth for the church (as a pastor for more than twenty years, I have come to realize that such formulas don't exist). I will, however, present an innovative approach to church evangelism that adds a new paradigm on the subject, and introduce ideas that, while common and practical to most Christians, might actually be shocking and reinvigorating to the local church. I truly believe this book reveals a concept of church evangelism that will unlock enormous doors to your community. Simply stated, this book provides the God-ordained promise of evangelism that, in many ways, is presently latent but easily attainable by any evangelical church. My earnest goal is not to reinvent the wheel but to show you how it can work more efficiently than ever imagined.

REACH was written to challenge Christian leaders to rethink the way they do church evangelism. Some churches are doing an incredible job in this area. However, many evangelical churches struggle to be effective change agents in their local communities. Each year thousands of evangelical churches fail to baptize even one convert to Christ. What's worse, every year over 2.5 million people pass from the face of the earth in the United States.[1] Now, consider this: Only God knows how many of those people who die will wind up in a state of damnation and separation from God for all eternity. Researchers in this area estimate that over 60 percent of these people will go into eternity without Christ.[2] Many of these people were denied the opportunity to learn about the saving grace and knowledge of Jesus Christ, because nobody took the time to introduce them to a living and eternal God. This sad but true commentary undermines the mandate of the gospel that says, "Go and make disciples of all nations, baptizing them in the name of the Father and of the Son and of the Holy Spirit, and teaching them to obey everything I have commanded you" (Matt. 28:19–20).

REACH Team is a dynamic approach to personal and corporate evangelism in the church for a new millennium. This book is based on what I have learned over twenty years of pastoral ministry, reflecting a combination of subtle successes as well as disastrous failures. Trust me when I say there are no easy answers. When you think about it, even Jesus realized that the evangelization of the world was not going to be easy. He instructed believers, "The harvest is plentiful but the workers are few. Ask the Lord of the harvest, therefore, to send out workers into his harvest field" (Matt. 9:37–38). Pastors and church leaders are praying daily for the Lord to "send out workers" from their churches into the harvest fields. The sad reality is, "the workers are few." Truth be known, every church leader desires to be a part of an evangelistically active church where every member is purposefully and intentionally reaching out to unchurched people. However, many churches have grown weary in their zeal for the Great Commission, and as a result, many pastors are uncertain how to lead others toward a new era of effective evangelization. When you combine apathetic church members with bewildered pastors, the results are devastating.

Even with the reality that church evangelism is not for the timid and weakhearted, I firmly believe that Jesus did not command the Christian community to fulfill an evangelization mandate that was simply "too hard" to carry out. Remember, a vital cog of the Great Commission is the personal promise of Jesus himself when he said, "And surely I am with you always, to the very end of the age" (Matt. 28:20). Also, just prior to his ascension into heaven, Jesus told his disciples, "But you will receive power when the Holy Spirit comes upon you; and you will be my witnesses in Jerusalem, and in all Judea and Samaria, and to the ends of the earth" (Acts 1:8). Think about it: Jesus promised he would be with us every step of the way and would give us the power to truly *be* witnesses worldwide. If that is true, then why is evangelization so hard for so many churches?

Maybe we (the church in general) have unintentionally made evangelism harder than it really is. Remember: Witnessing is simply sharing what we know of Jesus with others. Believers can start where they are with what they know. The primary factor is to love Jesus and to love others. If we love Jesus and we love people, we will do our best to bring the two together.

I've come to realize that most believers truly desire to impact the kingdom of God through the winning of souls. As Bill Hybels once wrote, "I think all true followers of Christ long to become contagious Christians."[3] Deep in their hearts, they realize nothing is greater than opening the hearts of the unsaved to the love and grace of Jesus Christ. Most Christians are just unsure about how to go about witnessing to their unchurched and unsaved family and friends.

All this brings me back to the question: What is REACH Team? REACH is an acronym that stands for the following:

- Relational
- Evangelism
- And
- Cultivational
- Hospitality

Let's take each word individually and attempt to break it down for further clarification and understanding.

Relational

In each church where I have served as pastor, one underlying element always aided in the unchurched coming to and staying connected to the church—relationships. Friends bringing friends to church; neighbors reaching out to other neighbors; work associates sharing with other work associates. Also (and very important), when a prospective person or family attended our church for the first time without an invitation from anyone, they were always more likely to return for future visits if they sensed a degree of friendliness and relationship-building potential from within the church. All of these people liked other things about the church—music services, preaching, youth programs, nursery provisions, and so on. Inevitably, however, the vast majority would either come or go based upon potential *relationships*. Regardless of how impersonal or indifferent we may think our society has become, people still seek meaningful relationships. In fact, most people are willing to let down their guard to discover new friendships. REACH Team is a program designed to train Christians in relationship-building principles. Readers of this book (and participants of the REACH program) will learn how to formulate relationships with their unchurched circle of influence. We'll address this issue more in chapter 1.

Evangelism

The key to REACH Team is its simple yet unique approach in teaching believers how to develop relationships that open doors to personal evangelistic encounters. For years I've heard church members say such things as, "Lost people don't want to hear the gospel," or "Unchurched people take offense when you bring up the name Jesus." Certainly, a segment of our population has hearts so hardened to the gospel that the mere mention of Jesus causes conflict or retaliation. Philosophical thought and such worldviews as postmodernism, modernity, empiricism, humanism, and existentialism flood our modern cultural landscape, creating an atmosphere of revolutionary diversity. This, however, should not alarm or detour the church from its evangelistic mandate. Remember what Jesus told his disciples when he sent them out to evangelize: "If anyone will not welcome you or listen to your words, shake the dust off your feet when you leave that home or town" (Matt. 10:14).

That being said, most researchers in the area of church growth concur that the majority of the unchurched in America are actually *interested* in spiritual matters. We often think of the unchurched as those who possess little if any interest in the church or rarely darken its doors. Yet this is simply not true. In his book *Surprising Insights from the Unchurched*, Thom Rainer states, "The word 'unchurched' naturally implies that a person has no interest in a church and never attends a church. Our survey of the formerly unchurched indicates, however, that relatively few Americans 'never' attend church. . . . If we defined an unchurched person as one who never attends any kind of church service in a year, including holiday services, the population of the unchurched in America would be small."[4] People are generally interested in the gospel of Jesus Christ. We must define, develop, and implement innovative ways of propagating the gospel.

And

I know what you're thinking: *Why spend time and space writing about a simple conjunction used hundreds of times in everyday conversation?* The word *and* in this acronym is more than just a conjunction to complete the word REACH. The word *and* connects the "how-to" concerning the strategy of relational evangelism. Although the concept of relational evangelism is depicted throughout the Bible, most evangelistic training tools focus primarily on *what* a person should share, yet often omit the *how, when,* and *where* of sharing one's faith. Remember this part of Paul's testimony to the church at Corinth: "Do not cause anyone to stumble, whether Jews, Greeks, or the church of God—even as I try to please everybody in every way. For I am not seeking my own good but the good of many, so that they may be saved" (1 Cor. 10:32–33). REACH Team attempts to mimic that evangelistic philosophy by training people in different methods of sharing their faith. The goal is for the people on the receiving end of these acts of hospitality to come away with a more positive attitude and a more favorable impression of Christianity and the church. One important nonnegotiable exists at this point: We never want to tamper with the *what* of the gospel message but we do need to examine the *how*. Entirely too many churches and church growth proponents have lowered the entrance requirements to faith in Jesus Christ in order to make the gospel more palatable. Ultimately, this type of approach will, if it hasn't already, backfire, thereby robbing the church of the power found within the gospel. Still, the church must not be fearful of exploring radical and creative approaches to establishing inroads with the unchurched.

Cultivational

Jesus said in John 4:35, "I tell you, open your eyes and look at the fields! For they are ripe for harvest." The impression of many church members today is that we have fewer and fewer prospects. In our church there is an ongoing question concerning those who visit our services: "Are they a prospect or a suspect?" Actually, every person we meet is a potential prospect, perhaps not for our church, but for our reaching out to establish a witnessing relationship. While it can be reasoned that unchurched people are not as likely to initiate an open encounter with the church, it certainly does not negate the fact that they are willing to establish meaningful relationships with those associated with the church. Therefore, the church must be about the business of cultivating relationships with the unchurched through acts of genuine hospitality.

We have a great message to share. But a great message doesn't amount to much if you don't have an audience that is listening. Years ago George Barna wrote a booklet entitled, "We Have Seen the Future: The Demise of Christianity in Los Angeles County."[5] He noted that even with the existence of numerous large, influential churches scattered throughout Los Angeles County, the church in general had all but lost its effect upon the secular community around them. He warned that if the church didn't change its strategy soon, this evident loss of influence would be witnessed all across America. What approach or method will capture the attention of the non-

Christian society around us? I propose that whatever manner you choose, the authoritative gospel is important. However, the primary mode for sharing the gospel should be a personal *demonstration of one's faith* so the watching world can see Christ and experience his divine love.

Hospitality

People today are far more protective of their personal and private time. George Barna points out that "unchurched people are not always 'people persons.' Some want a church that is a caring community, but they are not especially willing to bend over backwards to fit the relational style they require of a congregation."[6] Barna goes on to say that one of the main reasons for the absence of the unchurched is that they have not been invited to participate. "The chances of unchurched people coming to worship services on their own, without soft but continual encouragement from trusted friends, is slim."[7]

Statistics show that in the first years of our new millennium, and especially following the terrorist attacks of September 11, 2001, a renewed interest in the Christian church has risen among the unchurched. More and more people who once possessed previous affiliations with the church have sought to deepen their faith again. However, the wide majority of these unchurched are looking to be *invited* to attend and participate with the church. In fact, unchurched people are more likely to respond to a personal invitation to attend church rather than external pressures such as media or marketing techniques. People in today's society look for authentic relationships. The approach must be personal, not pushy or coercing. The unchurched want to "see" that the faith Christianity propagates is substantive.

That is where acts of hospitality and kindness come in. As the old saying goes, "People would rather see a sermon than hear one." This world is crying out to *see* more sermons preached. Seeing the love of God in action strikes a cord deep inside the unchurched. I am reminded of these words of Jesus: "By this all men will know that you are my disciples, if you love one another" (John 13:35). Jesus was known as a "suffering Servant." The waiting world of Jesus's day longed for a king and a ruler, not a lowly servant. He fed the hungry, healed the sick, taught the unlearned, and loved the outcast. God obviously understands that humility is one of the keys to attracting the attention of the unchurched. We have searched the world for effective evangelism programs, but perhaps the most obvious one has been right in front of our faces all along—performing humble acts of hospitality that will cause the unchurched world to notice our deeds and listen to God's message.

REACH Team is actually several ministry approaches all rolled into one interesting package. Perhaps the easiest way to explain REACH Team is to define and understand the word *hybrid*. Now, bear with me; while I was never raised on a farm, I did grow up in the bluegrass of Kentucky, and I recently lived in the "Hoosier" state of Indiana, both known for their agricultural efforts. *Hybrid* is a genetic term relating to something of mixed origin or composition, often used in the world of agriculture. Hybrid is also what REACH Team is all about, a conglomeration of successful ministry and evangelism strategies the church has been implementing for numerous years. REACH Team includes all of the following:

- Intentional evangelism—personally sharing one's faith one-on-one.
- Relational or friendship evangelism—cultivating friendships as a bridge to sharing the gospel.
- Family evangelism—sharing one's faith with personal and extended family members.
- Event evangelism—inviting the unchurched to attend special events and activities.
- Servant evangelism—efforts of servitude that open doors to evangelistic opportunities with the unchurched.

The Uniqueness of a "Team" Approach

Perhaps the one overriding key to REACH Team is its team approach to evangelism. Most evangelistic programs teach Christians how to share their faith with the unchurched. Other programs specialize in teaching Christians how to establish relationships with the unchurched. A few even focus on showing Christians how to perform random acts of kindness. However, in all of these programs, participation is based primarily on *individuality*. In other words, success is based upon what you do individually with your prospect or unchurched acquaintance. I've discovered that church members perform more efficiently as a group or team rather than separately or individually. In fact, I think that basic philosophy is true in most areas. Granted, Microsoft would not be where it is today without Bill Gates, yet even Bill Gates will tell you that he could not have accomplished all that Microsoft has become by himself. Great individual athletes like Michael Jordan, Wayne Gretzky, or Joe Montana will all attest that championships are won by teams, not individuals. True, we idolize the Rambos, Rockys, and Terminators of the silver screen for their individual strength. Yet, truth be known, virtually nothing was ever accomplished based on an individual acting alone. Even the Lone Ranger had Tonto riding with him everywhere he went!

We will further discuss the team approach in chapter 2; however, I do want to share another acronym used to define REACH Team:

- Together
- Everybody
- Accomplishes
- More

People by nature depend upon one another. We gain valuable support and encouragement from our relationships. An old Chinese proverb states, "Behind an able man there are always other able men." At the heart of great and unprecedented achievement is the concept of *team*. This is a unique proponent of REACH Team. Individuals work together while attempting to reach the unchurched. Team members keep one another accountable, encouraged, motivated, and involved. The team approach allows all individuals, regardless of their spiritual gifts, to have meaningful participation in evangelistic efforts. Think about it: Church members with the gifts of hospitality, giving, mercy, administration, and so on all work together to establish meaningful encounters with the unchurched.

Neither an academic theorist nor a profound theologian has written this book. While I attempt to bring theory and theology to the content, my primary purpose for this work is to be practical and applicable to churches of all shapes and sizes. My sole motivation is to attempt to revive evangelistic activity among many dead and dying churches across America. Now more than ever the church must be about the business of reaching souls for the kingdom. I can only pray that as you read the pages of this book, your heart will become stirred with the possibilities and opportunities of touching the hearts and lives of the unchurched around us.

PART 1

Introducing the Philosophy of REACH Team

1

The Relational Approach to Evangelism

It was a beautiful late-spring afternoon in central Indiana. The air was cool, crisp, and refreshing. My family had moved into a new neighborhood a few months earlier. After dinner, we decided to take a family bicycle ride around the community. As we rode through the streets, we came to a local park. Needless to say, our children insisted that we stop for a while. While the kids played, my wife, Patty, and I stood by our bicycles close to the road and talked.

Within a few minutes, another family rode up on their bicycles. We greeted them as they stopped and exchanged introductions and pleasantries. Their only child at that time, Channing, was a little timid to walk over to the playground area by herself, so Patty called our middle child, Hannah, over to where we were standing and introduced the girls to one another. They immediately struck up a friendship and hurried off to the playground area. Jeff and Jenny Gabe thanked us for including their daughter with our children. We continued a casual conversation for about thirty minutes. I found out that Jeff was an avid golfer and even had a business at one time repairing golf clubs. (How great is this—a complete "hacker" like me having a new friend who repairs golf clubs!) "Wow, that's great," I said. "I love to play golf. Maybe we can get together and play a round sometime?" He replied, "Are you serious? I'd love to! How soon can you go?" Patty and Jenny talked about color patterns and other decorating ideas for their new homes. We found out that the Gabes had been in their home for a short while as well and lived on the street directly behind our cul-de-sac. In fact, our backyards backed up to one another.

As we began to prepare for our trip home, Jeff asked me what I did for a living. *Oh no*, I thought, *when I tell him I'm a pastor, he's going to think that the only reason Patty and I were kind to them was to "recruit" them as new members!* Yet I realized that if this friendship was to last, transparency was a must. So I said, "I'm the pastor at Fall Creek Baptist Church a few miles from here." A look of astonishment came upon Jeff's face. He turned and looked at Jenny with that same stunned expression. *We're doomed*, I thought. Then Jeff said, "I can't believe it. We've been looking for a new church home for months and haven't found a place to worship. Would it be okay to come and visit sometime?" "Would it be okay? . . . Why, it would be awesome." Jeff, Jenny, and Channing were in our church the following Sunday, and they haven't missed too many Sundays since. Jeff and Jenny joined our church, and Channing made a profession of faith and was baptized. That was four years ago, and we remain good friends and neighbors.

Establishing Relationships with the Unchurched Is Vital to Effective Church Growth

I learned something from that first encounter with our neighbors. Through the years, I have invited hundreds of people to church. I've spearheaded high-attendance campaigns for my churches, urged people to invite their friends and neighbors to church, and mailed thousands of slick advertising cards offering invitations to people in the surrounding church area. What made this encounter with the Gabe family so different from countless other invitations? We established a relationship.

The unchurched may be drawn to a church by a particular type of music, preaching style, ministry opportunity, or even something as basic as a schedule of events. Surprisingly, I discovered recently in a survey conducted by the Rainer Group that 58 percent of all people surveyed are primarily interested in the doctrine/theology of the church. However, in that same survey, 53 percent of the people said that the second most important element about selecting a church was people caring for others, and another 45 percent said that the fourth most important element was the friendliness of the people within that church.[1] Charles Arn has done excellent work related to researching the attitudes and opinions of the unchurched. Notice his results as to why the previously unchurched connect with a church:[2]

Special need	1–2 percent
Walk in	2–3 percent
Visitation	1–2 percent
Church program	2–3 percent
Mass evangelism	0–5 percent
Sunday school	4–5 percent
Pastor/staff	1–6 percent
Friendship/relative	75–90 percent

In recent years, I've begun to ask new members what attracted them to our church. Overwhelmingly, virtually all of them have said that our church is friendly and full of kind, considerate people. Most of these new members felt a sense of belonging. They connected to our church through people and relationships. Recently I had lunch with a prospective family who has been visiting our church. I asked them, "What about our church appeals most to you?" Without hesitation, the husband said, "Pastor, being in the military, we have moved numerous times over the last fourteen years. In fact, during that time, we have attended over nineteen different churches. What we like most about your church is the friendliness and warmth of the people. We've never attended a church that made us feel so welcome before." Because of his response, I began to think, *How can we harness this attraction into a ministry of reaching out to the unchurched?*

I've found that most unchurched people are looking for meaningful relationships. I'm not suggesting that they are miserable or completely unhappy. To the contrary, most are energetic, aggressive, and driven. They have achieved something with their lives—at least according to the world's standards. However, a hard-charging lifestyle has left many of them weary from stress and meaningless relationships, thereby motivating them to look elsewhere for significance and purpose. Still, not all unchurched people think God or Christianity will help them overcome such struggles. If that were the case, our churches would be running over every Sunday. I truly believe that the unchurched are searching, looking for the answers to life that have thus far evaded them. Many of those unchurched people will find answers to their questions by Christians reaching out and establishing meaningful relationships with them.

An important part of the relational philosophy of REACH Team is intentional acts of hospitality, which will create friendships that will open doors to evangelistic opportunities. As we demonstrate authentic, genuine compassion for the unchurched, they will see and experience the love of God. Remember: The mere offer to help and love people unconditionally holds great power!

Jesus Built Evangelistic Relationships

This book is not simply about evangelism but about allowing the presence of Jesus Christ within us to affect those around us. One of Jesus's greatest attributes was his love and unconditional acceptance of people. Look at his band of followers. They were not the social elite; they were common, poor, and ordinary. Even his twelve disciples were of no prized disposition. They were smelly fishermen, tax collectors, and foreigners from different cultural backgrounds. Yet he loved and nurtured them all. Whether harlots, lepers, beggars, or thieves who hung next to him on the cross, Jesus related to everyone who came to him. One of the greatest accolades to Jesus's earthly mission is this verse: "[Jesus is] a friend of tax collectors and 'sinners'" (Matt. 11:19).

It's sad to ponder, but I wonder, if Jesus appeared on earth today, how many churches would accept him as a member? Why? Jesus would have been questionable membership material for most churches because he ran with the wrong crowd. The people who were shunned by religious types were those who kept seeking him out. When nonbelievers came to him, Jesus welcomed them heartily and often enjoyed dinner or fellowship with them. Socializing with the social outcasts of his day ruined Jesus's credibility with the religious crowd. Still, Jesus went out of his way to cultivate those relationships. If we are serious about reaching our generation of unchurched people, we must do the same thing. As was true with Jesus, we too find that words, actions, deeds, or a compassionate touch can be powerful tools to convey God's unconditional grace.

Jesus is our model for personal evangelism. Many of his encounters, such as those with Nicodemus, Bartimaeus, Zachaeus, and the woman at the well, were relational. However, the time required to establish a witnessing relationship will vary with the person, the preparatory work already done by others, and the work of the Holy Spirit. The relationship necessary to lead a person to Christ may require three years, three months, or three minutes. Each is unique. No two of Jesus's encounters were the same, nor will ours all be the same.

Experts in church growth tell us that relational (friendship or lifestyle) evangelism is the most widely practiced evangelistic approach among the laity in the church today. Some have estimated that more than eight out of ten church members prefer the relational approach of evangelism.[3] The problem with this approach is that it is perhaps the most loosely defined and structured approach the church implements. Relational evangelism is often criticized as a soft-sell strategy that takes extra time, effort, and energy yet holds little accountability on the part of the Christian witness. For instance, instead of aggressively pursuing evangelistic opportunities, Christians often convince themselves that if they live a good life and are friendly to all people, then God will take care of the rest.

In contrast, REACH Team is all about "showing" and "telling" people the love of Jesus. Paul wrote to the Christians in Rome, "How, then, can they call on the one they have not believed in? And how can they believe in the one of whom they have not heard? And how can they hear without someone preaching to them? And how can they preach unless they are sent? As it is written, 'How beautiful are the feet of those who bring good news!'" (Rom. 10:14–15). We must show the unchurched the love of Jesus Christ so we might have opportunity to tell them the Good News. It is not an either/or proposition but a both/and.

Relational evangelism is demonstrated through acts of kindness. For instance, consider the biblical story of the demoniac whom Jesus healed, and as a result, he chose to follow Jesus. To his inquiry Jesus replied, "Return home and tell how much God has done for you" (Luke 8:39). People who knew the demoniac saw a difference as a result of his encounter with Jesus. What he did and said showed onlookers that he had been with Jesus. In the same way, we are to show and then tell, naturally and consistently. Our testimony should be clearly presented and convey what Christ has done and means to us. In the clearest sense, it should be the inimitable authenticity of our faith demonstrated as a result of our profound and life-changing encounter with Jesus Christ.

Joe Aldrich describes relational or lifestyle evangelism as a three-step process. First, you must have a significant presence—relationship—in the life of the unchurched person. In the vast majority of cases, the unchurched will not listen to the gospel until they see and feel the love on which the gospel is based. Keep in mind, making a place in your life for unchurched people demands effort, thought, and, at times, risk. Bridges are harder to construct than walls. Realistically, we must embrace the fact that not all Christians attract as easily as others. Like a magnet, some repel instead of attract. Yet Christians alive to God—loving, caring, sharing, laughing, and embracing at the point of people's needs—present an unmistakable witness for Christ in their society.

Second, you must be able to present the gospel verbally. No matter how appealing or intriguing your lifestyle may be, the underlying reason will not become clear to the unchurched unless your faith in Christ is explained. A recent survey conducted by the Rainer Group indicated that 65 percent of all previously unchurched people were in fact witnessed to personally by a churchgoing Christian before actually joining a church themselves. Rainer also notes that while the seeker-sensitive movement has been a needed wake-up call for the declining church, some churches who have embraced the movement have actually experienced a decline in personal evangelistic efforts when the church focused solely on seeker sensitivity. In many cases, such a focus is viewed as the only method of effective evangelism.[4]

This is why REACH Team teaches not only relationship building but also evangelistic sharing. No one is "good enough" to let his or her life speak solely for Christ. The personal propagation of the gospel is necessary to point beyond oneself to Christ. Granted, when love is felt, the message is heard. However, I believe that personal lifestyle void of a proper proclamation of the gospel is an extreme to be avoided.

Third, Aldrich points out that the unchurched person may be persuaded to accept Jesus—that is, to make a commitment to Christ—if the prior two steps seem real and the prospects of becoming a Christian appear worthwhile.[5]

North Point Community Church in Alpharetta, Georgia, is one of the fastest-growing churches in North America. According to founding pastor Andy Stanley, its evangelistic strategy can be summed up in two words: *invest* and *invite*. Stanley sums up this strategic approach by saying, "From the beginning, we've told our people that our desire is to partner with them in the process of evangelism. As I am fond of saying, 'We will do what you are afraid or unequipped to do: raise the issues. You do what we cannot do: invite your friends.' As a result of this partnership, we see a high percentage of our people participating in personal evangelism. More than 90 percent of the adults we baptize came to NPCC at the invitation of a friend."[6]

I agree wholeheartedly with the "invest and invite" strategy. However, I think one potential issue in the "invest and invite" strategy has been overlooked—not everyone you invite to church will readily attend. Therefore, if the unchurched refuse to attend, do we cut them off completely and move to the next person? I certainly hope not. Just because some unchurched people refuse to attend a church-sponsored function is no reason to write them off. Allow me to take a liberty with the "invest and invite" strategy by adding one additional step to the process—*introduce*. At times the only way an unchurched person will hear the gospel is through your "own personal appeal" (introduction), even when you have invested valuable time with them and invited them repeatedly to church activities (see 2 Tim. 4:1–2).

Such was the case with Terry and Pam O'Quinn. My first pastorate after seminary was in Brunswick, Georgia. After a few months on the field, Patty and I bought our first home. We were thrilled. While the house was being built, we would go by every afternoon to inspect the progress. One afternoon, we heard someone call out, "Anybody home?" Although we did not recognize the voice, we assumed it was someone from our church who stopped by to see the house. As Terry and Pam entered our home, we were startled at first, having never been introduced. "Hello, can I help you?" (That's Southern for "What are you doing here?") "No," Terry replied, "we just came by to welcome you to the neighborhood." We introduced ourselves and shared some small talk. Terry told me that he was a home contractor and would love to help me with any work I would be doing on the house. I thought, *This is great. I guess this is what you call Southern hospitality.* I took Terry up on his offer, and he helped put on all of our doors and trim work. Needless to say, we began a genuine friendship.

Over the next several months, Patty and I invited Terry and Pam to our church repeatedly, but they would never attend. In one sense, it was a strange relationship. For instance, almost daily we would stand in our driveways talking and laughing. Terry installed a basketball hoop for his two teenage sons, and I found myself playing basketball at their house three and four times a week. We had cookouts, went fishing together, went to movies and restaurants, and played cards. Our friendship grew by leaps and bounds. Yet even though they knew (and readily accepted) that I was a pastor, they never accepted our consistent invitation to attend church. We were somewhat baffled by their refusal to attend church, yet we continued in our newfound relationship.

After a few more months went by, I became more and more convicted about not coming right out and sharing my faith with Terry and Pam. After all, I was constantly challenging my congregation to share their faith with their friends. It was time for me to practice what I preached. Late one afternoon, I looked out my front family-room window and saw Terry cutting some wood to burn in his fireplace. I walked over to his house and began a casual conversation. Finally, after several minutes of chitchat, I gathered my courage and said, "Terry, Patty and I have noticed that your family doesn't attend a church regularly, and that you have never accepted our invitation to attend our church. Is there a reason why you won't go to church with us?"

Little did I realize at the time, but I had just asked what some evangelism practitioners call a "key or inquiry question." In other words, a lead-in question that serves to initiate an evangelistic conversation. Terry looked up at me, paused for a moment, and set his ax down. (Needless to say, I was relieved when he did that!) He had a sheepish grin on his face and said nervously, "I was wondering when you were going to ask me that question." He proceeded to tell me about his early life attending church with his family. He said that his family had been wounded by certain events that had transpired in their former church and never regained confidence in the church again. He went on to say that they had been considering our invitation for some time but simply weren't ready. I told Patty about our conversation and we both agreed to remain steadfast in the friendship but to not put quite as much pressure on Terry and Pam about attending our church. We also committed ourselves to pray daily for their salvation and church participation.

After more than a year had gone by since we first met Terry and Pam, our friendship was as strong and encouraging as ever. Patty and I were able to talk to them about the Lord with greater freedom, yet we were careful not to push too hard. Eventually, I witnessed to Terry, Pam, and their two sons, and they all professed faith in Jesus Christ. They began attending our church on a regular basis, as did some of their extended family members and friends. All together, more than twenty people began attending our church as a direct result of that one cultivated relationship. However, two things about that encounter are important to remember: First, it took energy and effort to cultivate the relationship over an extended period of time. Second, Patty and I invested a lot of time with the O'Quinns in order to see the doors open to talk to (instruct) them about the gospel message of Jesus Christ. Had we never developed a close friendship, we would have never had the wonderful opportunity of seeing that entire family come to Christ.

Are You Establishing Evangelistic Relationships with Unchurched People?

Not long ago I shared a series of sermons focusing on the subject of building evangelistic relationships. As it turned out, the series inspired many within our church to concentrate more on reaching out to their unchurched neighbors, work associates, and friends. The following is a story from one of our newly motivated church members:

> I have become very good friends with a co-worker over the last five years. I began witnessing to her over four years ago. As time went on (and I felt more comfortable) I got bolder in my witnessing. Within the last year she has initiated many spiritual talks with me! For four years she was polite but "not interested." This is not to say that I didn't get discouraged. At times I thought this was futile. But as you continued to preach more and more about truly caring for those around us, I just started praying that God would work in spite of me. I learned to get out of the way and let God work. Long story short, I asked her again last week to come to church with me. Without batting an eye she said, "Sure!" She even asked if she could bring her daughter! After five years.

God never intended for church members to sit in the church pews while paying the ministerial staff to do the ministry of the church. As a follower of Jesus Christ, each believer is called and commissioned to be salt and light in all situations. Every day is a new and exciting opportunity to share the love of God with a lost and dying world. Every Christian possesses a personal testimony, therefore every encounter we have with the unchurched is unique. In other words, we are to use our unique abilities, personalities, and opportunities that God has given us to draw others to the Savior. Think about it: There were certain people whom Peter, a common fisherman, could reach whom Paul, an educated Pharisee, could never reach. A businessman like Barnabas could reach some people tax collectors such as Matthew or Zacchaeus could never relate to. Luke, a historian and doctor, could witness to some people whom John Mark, a youthful missionary, could never approach. God had a special audience for each of these men. God has a special audience for you too.

Evangelism is often a process, a spiritual continuum between the one sharing his faith and the one being witnessed to. Some churches still view evangelism solely as a "one-shot" deal, meaning that you've got to let them have it while you've got their attention. This kind of attitude reveals a harvest mentality without any thought of proper cultivation, a crusade or revival effort, a one-on-one personal encounter, where Christians often feel that they've only got one opportunity to share the gospel. We need to think of evangelism not as a onetime project but rather as a continuous process. Paul wrote, "I planted the seed, Apollos watered it, but God made it grow" (1 Cor. 3:6). Any good Indiana farmer will tell you that you don't just drop seeds in the ground and expect a bumper crop. You've got to cultivate the soil, fertilize the crop, use proper insecticides to protect the crop, and hopefully receive proper amounts of water and sunshine.

The same principle is true in sharing our faith with the unchurched. Hearts that have been closed to the gospel will not always open up spontaneously. Dr. Paul Benjamin discovered this truth as a result of interviewing hundreds of people who came to Christ in the early 1970s. In his book *The Equipping Ministry*, he states that the average unchurched person requires five significant encounters with the gospel before accepting Jesus Christ as Savior.[7] Benjamin defines a "significant encounter" as one in which a person actually hears the message of God's love in such a way that it registers in his or her heart. Stop reading for a minute and ask yourself this question: What personal relationship with an unchurched person am I presently cultivating? Who needs to *see and experience* the love of God through me?

2

The Team Approach
to Evangelism

The year was 1904. It was a hot, sticky day at the World's Fair in St. Louis, Missouri. Hundreds of thousands of people had been walking in the hot sun for hours and were looking for something to cool them off. Arnold Fornachou had set up a booth selling frosty cold ice cream. Needless to say, the ice cream was an instant hit. In fact, it was so popular that Fornachou ran out of paper bowls and was left with nothing in which to serve his ice cream. At that point of desperation, an unlikely partner emerged to save the day—Ernest Hamwi, a pastry chef who had grown up in Damascus, Syria. In a nearby booth, he was selling a waffle-thin Persian confection called a *zalabia*. Unfortunately nobody was interested in his pastry delight.

When Ernest saw his neighbor's dilemma, he had a terrific idea. Taking a freshly cooked *zalabia* in hand, Ernest twisted it into a cornucopia shape and rolled it in sugar. Then he ran over to Fornachou's booth and offered it to him as a remedy to his plight. Fornachou didn't quite understand what he had in mind, so Ernest scooped up some ice cream, placed it atop the confection cone, and handed it to a waiting customer. Fornachou instantly got the message. A huge smile burst across his face, and in no time the two men were working together as a team—Ernest made edible cones, and Fornachou scooped ice cream. Back then the ingenious creation was called a "cornucopia," and it was the rage of the fair. Today we simply call it an ice-cream cone (and it's still a hit).[1] Teamwork has a way of making the impossible a reality, not to mention a great success!

When I think of the church in its role and responsibility of reaching our lost world with the gospel, I naturally think of a team approach. Such an approach to evangelism is nothing earth-shattering or novel. Throughout the New Testament, we find numerous examples of two or more individuals going out and working together as a team to share their faith. Matthew 9–10 tells us that Jesus had been going through all the towns and villages teaching and preaching about the kingdom of God. The spectacular nature of Jesus's ministry attracted large crowds. Matthew 9:36 reveals that when Jesus saw the large crowd, "he had compassion on them because they were harassed and helpless, like sheep without a shepherd." As a result of seeing the terrible plight of the people, Jesus instructed his disciples to pray to the Father concerning the great harvest of souls: "The harvest is plentiful but the workers are few. Ask the Lord of the harvest, therefore, to send out workers into his harvest field" (Matt. 9:37–38).

Jesus sent his disciples out and gave them authority to preach and minister the gospel to the *lost sheep of Israel*. Interestingly, the Twelve were sent out in teams of two (Mark 6:7). Jesus goes on to explain the procedure of their evangelistic efforts through the remainder of Mark 6. These words of the Lord undoubtedly had an application beyond his own lifetime. The team approach was more fully demonstrated in the apostles' lives after the day of Pentecost (see Acts 2) in spreading the gospel within and outside of the newly established church.

Not only did Jesus send his disciples out as teams, he also worked with them as a team. For instance, the feeding of the five thousand, recorded in all four Gospel accounts. After Jesus had preached to the multitudes, it was late in the day, and the disciples wanted to send the people away rather than take on the responsibility of feeding them. However, Jesus took this opportunity to teach his disciples an important lesson in teamwork through acts of relational evangelism and hospitality. Rather than sending the people away, Jesus told the disciples to take inventory of their food. They discovered five loaves of bread and two fish, a meager amount considering the enormous size of the crowd. Nonetheless, in Jesus's hands, a miracle occurred. The bread and fish continually multiplied, enabling Jesus and his disciples to minister to everyone present.

The significance of this miracle was intended primarily for the disciples. Jesus illustrated the kind of ministry they would have after his departure. He showed the disciples that people had two needs—their spiritual need and their physical need. In order to open the hearts of the people to the gospel, Jesus sought to meet their physical needs, thereby establishing a compassionate framework from which to minister. Jesus taught the disciples the importance of working as a team to accomplish more for the kingdom. Keep in mind this repeated truth: *Team* means Together Everybody Accomplishes More! Mobilizing your church to work together in teams will only serve to enhance the overall evangelistic effort of your church.

The Small-Group Advantage

By developing REACH Teams, small groups work to cultivate and develop friendships with the unchurched through relationship-building activities and intentional acts of hospitality, which enhances the church's evangelistic effort. In fact, John Mark Terry writes that small groups actually possess some great advantages in relationship building and evangelistic sharing.[2]

The Small-Group Setting Is Nonthreatening

Many unchurched people feel intimidated by church buildings. However, a restaurant, bowling alley, city park, or even someone's family room is not threatening to them. A few years ago, Patty and I began hosting "discovery dinners" in our home. We invited prospects and guests who had made some type of contact with our church to our home for a meal and time of fellowship. I was amazed with how many people said they had never been in a minister's home. When these unchurched people enter our home, they realize that we are just like them; we have the same type of furniture, serve the same type of foods, and even have a television! Needless to say, within a few minutes our guests become relaxed and begin to unwind. After we finish dinner, we all sit in the family room and just get to know one another. I don't preach to them or dominate the conversation talking about the church. Amazingly, our guests sense our relaxed lifestyle and become more open and transparent themselves.

No Special Facility Is Required

Small groups have the luxury of cultivating relationships in a variety of locations, events, or facilities. My REACH Team likes to go out to dinner. Therefore, we often invite unchurched prospects to dine with us at local restaurants. It provides a comfortable, nonthreatening atmosphere.

A Casual Atmosphere Is Attractive and Appealing

Small groups don't require any special knowledge or clothing. Some people hesitate to attend a church or small group because they don't know what to do or wear. I realize that every church is different; some churches tend to be more formal in their attire. Our church, comprised predominately of twenty-to-forty-year-olds, has adopted a modest but casual attire. In fact, during warmer months, it is not uncommon for people to wear shorts and T-shirts.

Small Groups Provide Intimacy

In small groups, people tend to relate to one another on a more personal level. People want to participate in a group where people know their names and miss them when they are absent. Crowds, even in a small church, intimidate many unchurched people. Small groups have a way of breaking down barriers and removing fearful atmospheres.

The Personal Interaction of a Small Group Allows People to Find Answers

Many unchurched people have questions about the Bible and other religious matters but are often too afraid to ask for fear of embarrassment. They cannot ask the preacher during the sermon, but they can ask someone in their small group, or in this case, on the REACH Team. Small-group interaction provides a setting that makes asking questions easy.

Small Groups Offer Flexible Scheduling

It would be hard to reschedule a worship service for five hundred members, but a small group can easily adjust its meeting time. People's schedules are busier than ever. With intentional evangelism programs that designate one night per week to visit, it is often impossible to find a prospective family at home due to their busy lifestyle. People committed to small-group evangelism can set appointments, schedule events, and plan activities that are convenient for everyone involved.

Small Groups Provide a Greater Atmosphere to Talk about Spiritual Matters

Because small groups offer the opportunity of intimacy and friendship, people open up much sooner with personal questions and issues they are dealing with on a deeper level. The key here is what I call "trust factors." Before a person will openly discuss his or her personal questions, that person wants to know if you, the listener, can be trusted.

Small Groups Provide a Good Foundation for Those Making Decisions for Christ

Leading someone to faith in the comfortable setting of one's home is much easier and far less threatening than in a large church setting. This is not to say that people cannot get saved in worship settings. However, for many people, the thought of a public invitation (a practice we follow in our church) can create fear and trepidation.

One of my favorite evangelistic stories is in the healing of the paralytic (see Matt. 9:1–9; Mark 2:3–12; Luke 5:18–26). Four men (a team) had a friend who was a paralytic. They took their afflicted friend to Jesus, who was teaching in Capernaum at Peter's house. The four friends carried the paralytic to Jesus on a mat. When they got to Peter's house, a large gathering blocked the entrance to the house. Like many Palestinian dwellings, this house probably had an outside stairway leading to a flat roof. The men climbed the stairs to the roof and began digging aggressively through it in an attempt to get their friend to Jesus. After digging through the roof, the four men lowered their friend to Jesus's feet. Jesus viewed the determined effort of the four as visible evidence of their faith in his power to heal their friend. He did not rebuke the interruption to his teaching but unexpectedly told the paralytic that his sins were forgiven. Jesus then proceeded to heal the afflicted man of his paralysis. Mark 2:5 is important as it relates to teamwork. Notice that it says, "When Jesus saw *their* faith . . ." (emphasis mine). Whose faith? Those compassionate men who brought their friend to Jesus. It took a team effort. Their faithful teamwork moved the heart and healing hand of the Savior.

Steps to Team Development

Teamwork doesn't transpire magically or haphazardly. In order for the *team* to succeed, it takes *work*. Perhaps the greatest collegiate basketball coach of all time, John Wooden, once said, "The man who puts the ball through the hoop has ten hands." His motto was, "The most important player when we win is the rest of the team." Building a team effort within the church body to perform evangelistic efforts also takes work. A genuine group dynamic must take place in order for the team to work favorably with one another. Every team goes through a process of development that aids in its overall success and unity.

Step 1: Relationship Development

Team members develop a sense of unity, intimacy, and trust. Individuals draw closer to one another and become more dependent upon each other. The dynamic of group chemistry begins to take place. When people have a mutual love, respect, and admiration for one another, coupled with a clear, defined direction, the result is solid friendships and lifelong relationships.

Step 2: Partnership Development

Members of the team begin to discover each other's unique gifts, talents, and abilities, and how each person can implement his or her giftedness within the group. Each team member discovers his or her area of contribution and support and then learns to apply it while complementing the gifts of other team members. A primary element to the success of this step is communication. Team members must become more transparent and open with their individual gifts and how they will complement the entire group and contribute to its purpose.

Step 3: Workmanship Development

All the pieces of the puzzle fit together. All the team members' gifts, talents, and abilities are resourced together in a cooperative fashion. Just as an engine has separate proponents that work in conjunction with others to produce firepower, so the proponents of a team collaborate in order to create an effective atmosphere of relationship building. This step is about industry and cooperation. The team must set as a priority the willingness to work together. The team should have some clearly defined goals set in place by this time.

Step 4: Companionship Development

This is the end result of fruitful labor and relationship building. Friendships are formulated, bonds are created, and trust is established. The desired goal is to achieve the initial objectives and goals set forth by the team and the overall program. Personal traits such as transparency, honesty, encouragement, and support are evidenced more readily.

The Essence of Community in Team Development

It is important to develop an attitude of community service within the team. After all, this is what REACH Team is all about. Remember the following truths as to why we should evangelize as a team.

1. *In many ways, we see that the church of the Lord Jesus Christ began its ministry with a team approach.* Jesus spent his earthly ministry pouring himself into the lives of twelve men (a team). These twelve men would become the nucleus that ultimately launched the New Testament church. They

worked together to plant churches, serve on missionary and preaching journeys, and disciple the masses.

2. Team evangelism helps to build unity among its participants. When people truly unite together as a group, a cohesive spirit develops. Look at sports teams. Often we even hear the team's "superstar" readily admit, "We could not have accomplished this goal without the efforts of the entire team." Someone has coined the phrase, "There is no *I* in the word *team*." Even the great apostle Paul, with all of his accomplishments, had men and women like Barnabas, Silas, Luke, John Mark, Priscilla, Timothy, Lydia, Aquila, and Apollos to help him in his daily task of propagating the gospel of Christ.

3. Corporate efforts of outreach serve to increase the spiritual aptitude of all involved. Christians who tend to sit on the sidelines and watch ministry take place often become dissatisfied and barren in their faith. Statistics prove that there is a much greater fallout rate for those who fail to assimilate into the church. Team efforts provide a basis for corporate and consistent involvement, not only in evangelism but other areas of church life as well.

4. The team approach to relational evangelism helps everyone feel a part of the witnessing effort. The average church member pictures evangelization as a one-on-one confrontational approach. While this method is certainly not outdated or ineffective, not everyone is comfortable with or capable of this type of approach. Over the years, numerous spokespersons in the area of personal evangelism have stated that only 10 percent of the average church membership possesses the "giftedness" of intentional evangelism. While that statistic may be accurate, it doesn't mean that the other 90 percent should throw in the towel and be excused from the responsibility of reaching the unchurched. Team evangelization requires more people within the church serving in a variety of ways to accomplish the goal of reaching the unchurched.

5. Opportunities for outreach often open up for teams that otherwise might not open up for individuals. The potential of developing more viable prospects is greater from a team or corporate approach than merely depending upon one individual. It has been noted that the average person has about five to eight areas of personal influence in his or her life. Within those designated areas, each person has a direct contact with an estimated three to five people who would be considered unchurched. Suddenly your prospects have multiplied dramatically.

6. *The impact of a team approach demonstrates greater potential to the watching community of unchurched people.* Relationship evangelism efforts performed through acts of hospitality draw greater attention from the unchurched because of their novelty. The culmination of these random events gives the impression that your church is everywhere in the community, when in reality, it may only be a small group that is making such a dramatic impact.

7. *The effort of a team approach reflects greater appeal to the character and nature of Jesus Christ.* Something about a group effort draws the attention of others. And in this case, when the unchurched see believers working, serving, and witnessing together for one central purpose, the result is a greater reflection upon the character of Jesus Christ. The apostle Paul described it this way: "For we are to God the aroma of Christ among those who are being saved and those who are perishing" (2 Cor. 2:15). The atmosphere of a group of dedicated and transparent believers portrays an indelible impression of Jesus Christ.

C. Gene Wilkes, in his book *Jesus on Leadership,* observed that the power of teams not only is viable in today's workplace but also was actually demonstrated and potent in biblical times. He asserts:

- Teams involve more people, thus affording more resources, ideas, and energy than would an individual.

- Teams maximize a leader's potential and minimize his weaknesses. Strengths and weaknesses are more exposed in individuals.
- Teams provide multiple perspectives on how to meet a need or reach a goal, thus devising several alternatives for each situation. Individual insight is seldom as broad and deep as a group's when it takes on a problem.
- Teams share the credit for victories and the blame for losses. This fosters genuine humility and authenticity within the group. Individuals take credit and blame alone. This often fosters a sense of pride or personal failure.
- Teams keep leaders accountable for the goal. Individuals connected to no one can change the goal without accountability or communication.
- Teams can simply do more than individuals.[3]

Have you seen the overall effect that teamwork manifests in your church? Does your church have a staff that utilizes shared responsibilities, a deacon or elder ministry that ministers corporately to the flock, a committee that utilizes all of its unique gifts, skills, and abilities? The same can be true with your church's evangelistic efforts. I dare you to implement a team strategy of relational evangelism in the life of your church. See if after just a few short weeks total involvement increases, the number of prospects grows, and the overall attitude of outreach improves drastically.

3

The Biblical Mandate
for Evangelism

Not long ago I was coaching in one of my son's baseball games. Prior to the start, the Little League officials had the boys line up on the first and third base lines and repeat the Pledge of Allegiance. I was amazed at the number of boys, all between the ages of nine and ten, who did not know the words to the pledge even though many of them still repeat it daily in their schools. I remember learning to repeat the pledge by memory as a little boy in elementary school. I must admit, at that time I didn't understand exactly what it meant. Since those early days, however, I have repeated it often, with my hand placed over my heart, signifying my affirmation and commitment to our nation and heritage. Since the tragedy that took place in our nation on September 11, 2001, many of us have said the Pledge of Allegiance with a new vigor, enthusiasm, and sense of appreciation.

When I examine the New Testament, and particularly the words of our Lord Jesus Christ, I think there is a spiritual "Pledge of Allegiance" when it comes to the role and responsibility of the body of Christ. This pledge is formulated primarily in two separate passages of Scripture, yet they have an unmistakable thread uniting them. The first part of this pledge is found in Matthew 22:37–39 and is known as the "greatest commandment." Jesus's reply summarized the entire Decalogue: "Love the Lord your God with all your heart and with all your soul and with all your mind" (v. 37; see also Deut. 6:5). He added that the second command was to "love your neighbor as yourself" (v. 39; see also Lev. 19:18). Within these two commandments resides part of the primary responsibility of the church—love God and love others. If we fail to love God, we fail to love others. And if we fail to love others, we ultimately fail at fulfilling the commandment to love.

The second part of this pledge is found in Matthew 28:19–20, known as the Great Commission. Jesus instructed his disciples to "go and make disciples of all nations." These were the final words our Lord Jesus echoed before his ascension into heaven. This, in and of itself, makes this passage all the more crucial. After all, Jesus's final instruction to the church was global evangelization. How are these two great passages interrelated? Simple: We, as the body, are called and commanded to love God. One of the ways we demonstrate that love for God is by loving others. And the primary way we show the love of God to others is by witnessing to them about God's love and grace. In essence, I reveal my abiding love for God by showing and telling my neighbor what God has done for me.

Why Don't More Christians Share Jesus?

Most committed Christians possess an adequate understanding of these two passages. I'm afraid, however, that too many Christians have become so familiar with them that we have forgotten what an awesome responsibility these two passages hold for the Christian community.

Indifferent Christians

There are several reasons why the church is failing to effectively reach the unchurched in our society. The first reason, while not primary, is perhaps the most frightening and disturbing. Some feel that a large percentage of people who sit in church pews each week could care less about those outside the church who are dying daily and going straight to hell. As a pastor I am quite concerned over the lack of urgency and vigor related to evangelizing the lost. Without question, a subtle, complacent, uneasy sense of satisfaction with the status quo permeates today's church. We know the words, language, lingo, and spiritual phrases that make us sound as if we're evangelistic in nature. We also have the tools, programs, and seminars available to carry out virtually any type of evangelistic ministry. But something is missing. Is our level of motivation lacking? Perhaps. Tony Evans may be on the right track when he writes:

> I'm afraid that too many Christians have become so familiar with our spiritual jargon that we have forgotten what an awesome concept making disciples really is. Jesus committed His entire enterprise for this age to the church—to people like you and me. What's more, He told us to take it to "all the nations." Discipleship is so big that when we are obedient to God and faithful in discipling people, the church will impact the world. . . . That's why we must keep evangelism front and center in the life of the church. If the church is going to grow by making disciples, we have to have people who are willing to go into the whole world as Christ's witnesses. That's one reason Jesus sent us the Holy Spirit (see Acts 1:8).[1]

Intimidated Christians

This leads to our second and primary reason why the church is failing to reach out to the unchurched community. It is found in a simple yet profound four letter word—*fear*. Two separate yet distinct and applicable interpretations can be made to this word as it relates to the church. First, some churches are afraid to share Jesus because of fear of change. I understand the ideology of the homogenous principle— people groups possess a natural affinity toward those of their own likeness. However, just because the color of a person's skin, or the language of a person's culture, or the tradition of a person's heritage is different, does that alleviate me from the mandate of sharing the gospel? Such differences should never hinder you or me from sharing the gospel message of grace and love. We don't stop people of different ethnicity from entering our public schools, places of employment, shopping centers, recreational facilities, or restaurants for fear that they might cause change. Why should the church of our Lord Jesus Christ be any different?

The second aspect of fear centers upon the general sense of trepidation many people feel when faced with the thought of sharing their faith. Do you ever freeze up in fear when faced with an opportunity to share your faith in Jesus Christ? Have you ever encountered a bad or embarrassing situation as a result of trying to witness to an unchurched person? I think we all feel hesitation, fear, and for some, even total panic when it comes to talking to the unchurched about Jesus.

Most of us feel at risk when we talk about Jesus. We put ourselves out on a limb and become vulnerable to rejection, ridicule, and retaliation. We know we're supposed to witness. We also know God wants to use us as his tools to reach the lost and unchurched. But we're afraid. Stuck between responsibility and timidity is no place to be. Yet most Christians find themselves there. And the sad scenario for many Christians is that they often choose to keep quiet, miss wonderful opportunities for sharing their faith, and then beat themselves up mentally about it for days, weeks, even months.

Second Timothy 1:7 tells us, "For God did not give us a spirit of timidity, but a spirit of power, of love and of self-discipline." Later we'll look at how God enables us to overcome intimidation and witness to others.

Intolerable Christians

I think there is a final reason why the church is failing to reach the community of unchurched people. We live in a "watching world," a world that is constantly observing the actions of others. The world watches when Christians love. Consequently, the world also sees when the church is at odds with one another. As a pastor I realize how important the corporate image of the local church is to its community, particularly as it relates to its evangelistic impact.

Many of our churches are full of professing believers who claim to believe the truth but are producing intolerable ugliness. These people cannot get along with one another. They fight, argue, gossip, become embittered, and migrate from church to church, spreading their pettiness like an uncontrollable virus. Instead of being ambassadors for Christ, they have become an embarrassment to Christ. We must realize that the church is a living organism; therefore, it is subject to sickness and disease. If the church becomes anemic, it fails to display the beauty and fragrance of Christ.

Joseph Aldrich noted two important reasons why anyone developing an evangelistic strategy must first look at the overall health of a church. First, he says, God is not in the business of placing healthy babies into sick incubators. In other words, dying and decaying churches that display intolerable dispositions stand little chance of appealing to or winning new converts. Second, he notes that the health of the church is critical to evangelism because personality is a product of relationships. People often mimic those they associate with.

New Christians begin to pick up the sinful, unappealing attitudes and expressions of intolerable church members.[2] As a result, one of two things usually occurs: The new convert either begins to mimic the actions of other church members or is repulsed by the intolerable actions and quickly removes himself or herself from the church altogether. What we need are healthy, happy, and holy churches fulfilling the responsibility of the church by displaying the beauty of Christ through their testimony.

In churches that implement an active outreach program, usually only a small percentage of the total membership participates. This lack of participation can ultimately result in unhealthy churches. Rick Warren, in his book *The Purpose-Driven Church*, wrote, "I believe you measure the health or strength of a church by its sending capacity rather than its seating capacity. Churches are in the sending business. One of the questions we must ask in evaluating a church's health is, 'How many people are being mobilized for the Great Commission?'"[3] Many of our churches today are considered unhealthy because they are predominantly inward focused. Virtually no input or interest is placed on budgeting, scheduling activities, or staffing in the area of outreach, evangelism, or mission objectives.

Many of our churches have adopted an unhealthy imbalance of prioritization between ministry within the body and mission outside the body. For most of these churches the balance tilts toward ministry within the body as its primary function. I'm amazed (and frightened) when I see such vast numbers of church members who are convinced their sole reason for existence is to edify themselves.

Keys to Accomplishing the Great Commandment and the Great Commission

Think about the early church in Jerusalem. In Acts 2 we see some clear characteristics of a church that sought to reach out to all humanity, regardless of social, ethnic, or economic standing. Notice the following characteristics:

1. The Church Received the Word: Edification

Acts 2:42 says, "They devoted themselves to the apostles' teaching." A growing church will always be a *learning* church. In fact, when a church ceases to learn, it ceases to live. These three thousand baby Christians were completely "sold out" to the study of God's Word. They possessed an authentic, genuine spiritual hunger for scriptural truth. The foundation for a healthy Christian is personal and corporate edification. The apostle Peter wrote, "Like newborn babies, crave pure spiritual milk, so that by it you may grow up in your salvation, now that you have tasted that the Lord is good" (1 Peter 2:2–3).

The key, however, is for a learning church to be a *living* church. In other words, the truth of God's Word must not only be hidden in our hearts but also practiced in our lives. James says it this way: "Do not merely listen to the word, and so deceive yourselves. Do what it says. Anyone who listens to the word but does not do what it says is like a man who looks at his face in a mirror and, after looking at himself, goes away and immediately forgets what he looks like. But the man who looks intently into the perfect law that gives freedom, and continues to do this, not forgetting what he has heard, but doing it—he will be blessed in what he does" (James 1:22–25). Remember: Educational impression minus missions expression leads to spiritual depression.

2. The Church Related Winsomely: Cooperation

Fellowship is so important to the church's overall function that it stands as one of the foundational activities. Acts 2:42 says, "They devoted themselves to the apostles' teaching and to the fellowship, to the breaking of bread." Interestingly, this kind of fellowship did not exist prior to the giving of the Holy Spirit at Pentecost. This is the first time the word *fellowship* is used in the New Testament writings. This word denotes some kind of sharing—either sharing something with another person, or sharing through the personal experience of another person.[4] Notice verses 44–46: "All the believers were together and had everything in common. Selling their possessions and goods, they gave to anyone as he had need. Every day they continued to meet together in the temple courts. They broke bread in their homes and ate together with glad and sincere hearts."

Perhaps the most pertinent example of this type of fellowship is found in 2 Corinthians 8:1–5. Here we see the Macedonian church begging for the opportunity to give an offering, even though they themselves were quite poor. Yet they determined to participate in the act of *koinonia* by giving to others who had need. Why did they long for such an opportunity? Notice 2 Corinthians 8:5: "And they did not do as we expected, but they gave themselves first to the Lord [fellowship with him] and then to us in keeping with God's will." That's true, biblical *koinonia*: fellowship with God that results in fellowship with others. When we are in a proper relationship with God, we will naturally desire to share our possessions and goods with others in need.

Proper fellowship within the congregation is imperative for any church that wants to reach out to the unchurched. Why is this so important? Because God's invisible reflection is revealed through the visible presence of loving, fellowshiping people. The Bible declares this basic truth: "Dear friends, since God so loved us, we also ought to love one another. No one has ever seen God; but if we love one another, God lives in us and his love is made complete in us" (1 John 4:11–12). Most people in the unchurched world view authentic fellowship within a church as a clear sign of the presence of God. Love is seen and felt, not just preached or talked about. As a result, authentic fellowship serves as a magnet to draw the unchurched into the fellowship of believers.

3. The Church Rejoiced through Worship: Celebration

In Acts 2, we see that the early church worshiped the Lord by the "breaking of bread" (Lord's Supper), "prayer," and "meeting together in the temple courts, and praising God" (vv. 42, 46–47). It should come as no surprise that the Jerusalem church was a joyful, praising church. Verse 46 reminds us that the people of the church had "glad" hearts. Their joyfulness was further recognized through their open praise. To praise God is to recite his wonderful works and attributes. The desire of the Jerusalem church was to exalt the Lord, and that produced unspeakable joy. Those who seek to bring glory to themselves will never know true joy. Real joy comes from honoring God and giving him all glory and praise. Paul echoed that truth to the church at Philippi: "If you have any encouragement from being united with Christ, if any comfort from his love, if any fellowship with the Spirit, if any tenderness and compassion, then make my joy complete by being like-minded, having the same love, being one in spirit and purpose" (Phil. 2:1–2).

How does proper worship produce effective evangelism? Although the unbeliever cannot truly worship, he can watch true believers worship God. The unbeliever can witness the genuine joy of the Lord in the heart and expression of the believer. Therefore, when an unbeliever watches authentic worship, it becomes a dynamic witness. This is exactly what happened at Pentecost during the inauguration of the Jerusalem church. Early in Acts 2 a small band of disciples are baptized and filled with the Spirit, and the apostle Peter begins to preach the Word of God with astonishing boldness. Acts 2:6 says that "a crowd came together in bewilderment." It had to be a big crowd because three thousand people were saved that day! That initial worship service was so dynamic that in verse 37 it says, "When the people heard this, they were cut to the heart and said to Peter and the other apostles, 'Brothers, what shall we do?'"

4. The Church Reached Out to the World: Evangelization

The final characteristic of the Jerusalem church was evangelism. In fact, effective, relational-driven evangelism fueled the ultimate impact of the first fellowship's spiritual duty and character. Notice in verse 47 that "the Lord added to their number daily those who were being saved."

True evangelism flows from the life of a healthy church. The Jerusalem church offers us substantial insight into what comprises a healthy, dynamic, growing church worthy of its name. Proper devotion and commitment to the foundational characteristics of the church, coupled with continued submission to the leadership and empowering of the Holy Spirit, results in producing a powerful and saving impact on the unchurched.

PART 2

IMPLEMENTING THE CONCEPT OF REACH TEAM

4

The How-To
of REACH Team Ministry,
Part 1

Implementing the Strategy

Perhaps the greatest frustration I have experienced during my pastoral tenure has been motivating Christians to share Jesus. I've heard every excuse in the book. Through my experience with this growing frustration, REACH Team evolved. This strategy overcomes many of the excuses people raise for not being involved in evangelism.

Evangelism That Is Attainable

The last thing I want to do is take potshots at any existing programs that train Christians in personal evangelism. Some outstanding tools have been developed over the years, which produced tremendous results. However, when as a pastor I attempted to implement one of these programs, I was often met with resistance, hesitancy, or rejection. Why, I would ask, are so many Christians unwilling to participate in an evangelistic training program? Virtually every time, the answer came back, "What you want me to learn, study, and memorize is entirely too much!" I must confess, when looking at some of the existing evangelism programs on the market today, most of them do contain an overabundance of material to learn.

This leads me to a simple question: "Have we made evangelism too hard?" After all, it's not rocket science. In fact, Jesus said that one need only be childlike to receive his message (see Luke 18:17). I've come to the conclusion that most Christians in today's church are simply not willing or able to commit to a program that demands ten to sixteen weeks of continuous training and involves extensive learning and memorization. The demands on people are so great they simply refuse to involve themselves in activities that create more stress in their already hectic lives. Through this I realized that people need simplified materials and tools, not because of their intellectual or spiritual development, but rather due to the limited time and resources they have in their lives.

Evangelism That Is Time Conscious

Another frustration I have dealt with over the years is getting people to show up for organized evangelistic visitation efforts. Like many pastors I have attempted to lead my churches in weekly visitation programs. For a while, church members would show up. However, after a period of time, fewer and fewer church members came. I began asking some of my parishioners why they stopped coming to weekly visitation. Over and over the response was, "Pastor, I am already over-committed as it is." Between work, home, recreation, school, and family responsibilities, people simply did not have enough time each week to show up for another scheduled event. And to make matters worse, I (as their pastor) created more pressure on many of these people by preaching on Sunday that they needed to devote more time to their families; then the next Sunday I would preach to those "uncommitted heathen" for not showing up for church visitation the previous week!

Through this process, I began to study how Jesus evangelized others. He never mandated a weekly program on his disciples. He modeled instead a lifestyle in practice. Jesus witnessed to people through his daily activities and encounters. I firmly believe that most truly born-again believers do desire to share Jesus. I also believe that truly born-again believers want to earn a living, raise a family, go on vacation, and be active in recreational programs and social events. Therefore, the key was developing a witnessing strategy that incorporated personal evangelism into one's daily life.

Evangelism That Is Personal

I also began to realize just how impersonal at times our evangelistic efforts were. A good portion of our evangelism was based on visits to individuals and families where the visitor did not know the persons being visited. As a result, many of our evangelistic visits were disasters. Prospective people refused to allow church members into their homes, not because they were unfriendly but largely because the prospects didn't know these people and were guarded. Our visitation effort began to dwindle due to so many unsuccessful encounters with prospects.

At the same time, when I made pastoral visits with prospective people, I heard them say, "Your church is one of the most friendly churches I've ever attended." Guests and prospects liked the preaching, music, and other aspects of our worship services, but what brought them back was the friendliness of our church. I began to ask, "How can we incorporate our friendliness (a vital attraction point of our church) into our outreach efforts?" I realized that the missing ingredient to our outreach efforts was relationship building. Prospects were not only looking for the gospel but for relationships where the gospel was lived out and expressed.

Evangelism That Is All-Inclusive

The missing ingredient to this developing equation was discovering *how* to get more people involved in the process of evangelism. Statistics show that over 70 percent of all evangelical churches do not have any kind of organized evangelism program. The majority of churches with an outreach program produce minimal participation from its parishioners. I noticed in our own church that we averaged about 5 percent of our total membership as regular participants in our outreach program. I quickly realized that the vast majority of our church was failing to perform one of the greatest commands in all Scripture, "Go and make disciples of all nations" (Matt. 28:19).

Church growth practitioners tend to believe that 10 percent of the average church membership possesses a spiritual giftedness toward evangelism.[1] Still, I didn't think that the other 90 percent were exempt from the responsibility to evangelize. Therefore, the key was to develop an evangelism program that increased the participation level of the church membership, especially with those who did not feel as if they had a natural affinity toward evangelism. This is how the *team* approach was developed. People gain greater strength, possess greater gifts, and share greater courage when they work together rather than separately. The key here was to allow people to discover their personal spiritual gifts, and then learn to implement their giftedness in evangelistic activities.

Evangelism that is attainable, personal, time conscious, and seeks total inclusion. That is what REACH Team seeks to accomplish. What has been the result in our church? Amazingly, we have gone from 5 percent participation to almost 50 percent participation. We have seen an increase in baptisms and additions to our church membership. And most of all, we have seen a greater interest in evangelism from our church membership. Our goal is to have 100 percent participation in REACH Team in a few years.

How to Launch a REACH Team Ministry in Your Church

1. Announce the Concept of REACH Team to Your Church Family

Start by implementing a three-step strategy to announce or introduce the REACH Team ministry: proclamation, communication, and invitation. The pastor introduces the concept of REACH Team through a series of teachings focusing on the church's responsibility to reach the harvest. Each message should challenge believers to make a commitment to sharing their faith and encourage listeners to consider making a personal commitment in the newly announced REACH Team. Provide commitment cards for indicating one's interest in the ministry.

Step 2 is proper communication. At least six weeks prior to the initial information and enlistment meeting, share announcements in all services and church publications. You do not need to explain the complete concept of REACH Team at this point. The key is to saturate all communication avenues with the news of an upcoming exciting outreach opportunity. Communicating the proposal of a new outreach ministry, along with a sermon series on evangelism, creates an atmosphere of awareness and anticipation.

The third step is extending an invitation to an information and enlistment meeting. This is *not* a training session but simply an informational meeting to explain the basic concepts of the ministry. In the introductory meeting, make sure to provide for the following needs: refreshments, child care, an introductory packet about REACH Team, and an opportunity to sign up for participation. Try to keep the meeting within one hour. The key is not to overwhelm those who attend with too much information up front. Let them know that while REACH Team calls for a personal commitment, it doesn't call for unrealistic requirements. Let them know that each person works with a team of participants that help and encourage one another. Inform them that memorization and study is minimal, complete training is accomplished in one seminar, and that participants are encouraged to attend a monthly celebration meeting.

2. Invite Participants to the REACH Team Training Meeting

This second stage is the actual enlistment of participants for the REACH Team ministry. This is done at the official training meeting. At this meeting, people are asked to make a firm commitment of their time and energy to the program. Families and individuals are also assigned to teams at the training meeting. *Note*: It is important that families are committed to the REACH Team concept before they are assigned to a team. Why? Because once the teams are assigned, they each need time to work together and formulate a strategy of cooperation. Formulating a cohesive group is very important to the success of the team.

3. Conduct the REACH Team Training Seminar

This is the equipping stage of REACH Team ministry. I strongly urge you to consider offering the training seminar in one setting. The material can easily be taught in two to three hours. The participant's guide is located in appendix 1. The key is to have every participating family or individual obtain a copy of the REACH Team book and read each chapter thoroughly. (It is best if each participant can read the book prior to the training session.) Remember: People are more apt to attend if the training is not extended over a period of weeks. Below is the schedule that we have found most successful:

6:00 p.m.	Welcome and snack supper served. (Child care provided for session)
6:30 p.m.	Begin session training
7:30 p.m.	Short break with refreshments
7:45 p.m.	Continue session training
9:30 p.m.	Training session completed

In order to begin at 6:00 p.m. on a weeknight, we have discovered that offering a free snack supper is vital for attendance. This is not a banquet meal. We usually serve soup, sandwiches, and a drink. During the 7:30 p.m. break time, we serve a dessert and drink. Providing child care is a must in order to secure good participation.

Each pastor/training seminar instructor can decide which gospel presentation the participants should attempt to learn (see chap. 11, "The Priority Involved: Sharing Jesus in a Simple Manner"). Regardless of the gospel presentation you teach, each participant should write out his or her personal testimony. If your church chooses a gospel presentation not provided in this book, simply add the team concept and the relational and hospitality evangelism aspects that are presented in REACH Team to your present evangelism program.

It is also important for every participant in REACH to discover his or her spiritual gifts. Keep in mind that God has equipped every believer with specific gifts in order to be used for his glory and for the increase of his kingdom. Many Christians have used the excuse that because they do not possess the "gift of evangelism" (a gift this author believes does not exist), they are excused or omitted from evangelistic efforts. This is a flimsy and fatal excuse. God has given all the spiritual gifts for the purpose of utilizing them not only within the body but also outside the body, for evangelism and the fulfillment of the Great Commission.[2]

71

4. Assign REACH Teams

Team assignment is a crucial part of the overall success of REACH. Therefore, some basic elements should be considered when placing individuals and families on teams.

Age. The age demographic of the team is important because it often serves to represent people's interest, family issues, and attitudes. For instance, the interest level, family background, and attitude of a sixty-year-old couple and a thirty-year-old couple are quite different. Therefore, seek commonality with team members' ages and the prospects that are assigned to each team.

Same Bible study or home cell group association. Team members should have a close association through either a Sunday school class, Bible study group, or home cell group. This is important for several reasons. First, this assures for continued communication among the group members. They will naturally see one another on a weekly basis through their existing association with an organized and ongoing Bible study group. Second, it allows for the team to invite their unchurched prospects to a Bible study or fellowship group that involves other team members. The unchurched person now has some established relationships with class or group members through the REACH Team. Third, it allows for future and continual follow-up and relationship building. As the unchurched person associates with the class or group, he or she will have the opportunity to establish other relationships outside the initial REACH Team. Therefore, when the unchurched person becomes an active member of the church, he or she is not abandoned or forgotten by the REACH Team and has established some meaningful relationships with others in the class or group who are outside the team.

Team members should know one another and share some common interests. Establishing and building on commonality is important for each team. Shared interests, established friendships, and common bonds help to create a cohesiveness within the team. That cohesive spirit will naturally spill over into the life of the unchurched person whom the team is attempting to reach.

A variety of spiritual gifts are important. It is important to make sure that each team is comprised of various spiritual gifts among its participants. In other words, every team member doesn't need the gift or office of evangelism as his or her primary spiritual gift. On the other hand, you don't want every team member to have the gift of helps, hospitality, or mercy as his or her primary gift. A variety of spiritual gifts helps expand the outreach and hospitality capability of each team.

Based on the basic elements mentioned above, begin assigning individual participants to teams. I recommend that the pastor or REACH Team coordinator perform the actual assigning of individuals/families to teams. This process helps to guard against the possibility of a team becoming cliquish or a personal social club. Keep in mind, you want to create unity within the team while maintaining an open, inclusive spirit among team members.

Make sure that each team has a designated team leader. Every team needs an assigned team leader who is responsible for coordinating the activities and efforts of the team. The team leader should also serve as the contact person between the pastor/REACH Team coordinator and his or her assigned team members. Ideally, the team leader will possess the spiritual gift of administration, hospitality, or helps. Because REACH Teams are responsible for relationship building through acts of hospitality, these areas of spiritual giftedness lead toward more effective ministry.

5. Begin Implementing the REACH Team Strategy

Once all of your participants have gone through the training seminar, each team is encouraged to begin implementing the REACH Team strategy. There are three important keys to a successful implementation launch. First, *make sure that prospects are assigned to each team.* Do not assign more than five prospects to a team at any given time. This is based upon the fact that you are attempting to build relationships. If too many prospects are assigned to a team, the result can be limited relationship building. Second, *make sure that each team participant has developed his or her circle of influence sheet* (see appendix 2). One key to a successful harvest is for team participants to begin thinking of unsaved and unchurched people they know. Challenging participants to develop their circle of influence is vital; the greatest number of unchurched prospects can be developed through this effort. Third, *plan an initial fellowship activity for the REACH Team and unchurched prospects.* The sooner the team gets to know its prospects, the better. Remember that building relationships, establishing trust and friendship, is paramount! The unchurched want to establish meaningful relationships. Let them know that you are genuinely concerned for their welfare and total being.

Monthly REACH Team Celebrations

I cannot recommend highly enough that you schedule a monthly REACH Team celebration time. Make this a priority on the church's calendar. Several important aspects are involved in monthly celebration meetings. First is *education.* It is necessary to continue the REACH Team training on an ongoing basis. Schedule about twenty minutes per meeting for teaching about issues related to evangelistic outreach or relationship building.

Second, REACH Team celebration meetings are for *motivation.* At some point, all participants will need encouragement to continue in their outreach work. Teams having success in their relationship-building process often help motivate other teams who are struggling. Teams also share ideas that have worked for them in hopes that those ideas might work for other teams as well.

Third is the need for *inspiration*. People are motivated and inspired by success stories. Each month, we allow time for teams to report on their progress. The success stories keep teams going. It reminds them that their work is not returning void, and that God will work in the process if they remain faithful.

A fourth reason is personal and corporate *prayer*. Spend time each meeting praying specifically for each unchurched prospect you are attempting to reach. Pray for each prospect's salvation, and for others who are already Christians to come and be a part of your church fellowship.

A final reason is *celebration*. Each month announce to all the teams the number of prospects who have made professions of faith and united with your church. Teams should be encouraged to celebrate when unchurched people are drawn into the church (see Ps. 126:5–6; Luke 15:6–7).

5

The How-To
of REACH Team Ministry,
Part 2

Conducting Acts of Hospitality

Recently the Lord led me and my family to start a new church in Lexington, Kentucky. Soon after I arrived I implemented the REACH Team strategy with our initial core group. We developed seven teams, a total of twenty-one families. One of the first things we did was perform a community act of kindness. All of our teams met on a Saturday afternoon at a large subdivision close to where we plan to locate the new church. We decided to go door-to-door handing out free lightbulbs to every household. Along with the lightbulbs, we handed out brochures describing our new church and inviting people to come and visit our worship services. On each package containing the lightbulbs was a note that read, "Spreading the 'Light' of the World through the Love of Jesus Christ."

All total, we visited over two thousand homes in about three hours. We received a number of comments from people concerning our activity. Some people were a little suspicious, others were cautious, but most were impressed by the fact that we weren't trying to sell them something but rather giving them something for free! The next day at our Sunday worship service, eleven families from that subdivision attended as a result of our efforts. Within six weeks after the event, a total of seventeen families visited our services. All because we were willing to sacrifice our time and energy to show people the love of Jesus Christ in a simple, hospitable way.

The Lord has given the church a mandate to love others outside the walls of the church. "When Jesus gave the Great Commission, he had in mind a family that could never be large enough to satisfy his inclusive heart. Unfortunately more often than not we've experienced the great omission. While not all churches are called to be large, we are all called to be growing. We are all called to have a dynamic relationship with our surrounding community."[1] Most churches do a decent job of ministering inward to those within the church. Sadly, few churches are doing anything to impact those outside the walls of the church. What a tragedy—especially when you consider the vast number of unchurched people who respond favorably to random acts of kindness and hospitality. One of the easiest and most rewarding outreach efforts the church can perform is community acts of hospitality.

Acts of Cultivational Hospitality in the Community

The goal of acts of hospitality is to saturate a community with numerous low-pressure, high-service projects in order to show the love of Jesus in practical ways. The servant atmosphere provides a natural arena for effective personal evangelism. Any age can participate and it requires little training. In fact, providing community acts of hospitality produces an entry-level opportunity for participation in both relational and intentional evangelism. This type of effort is more than a social ministry. It is the firstfruits of effective evangelism.

We encourage each REACH Team to participate in some type of community random act of hospitality every six to eight weeks. Each team selects their activity.[2] We ask that each team fill out a community outreach report sheet and turn it in to our REACH Team coordinator at the completion of the event. The community outreach reports offer information concerning what type of event was conducted, the location, the target audience, and the estimated number of people reached. Sometimes several of our teams work together to perform a larger community project. Involving several teams cuts down on time, resources needed, and availability of people, and can increase the potential number of people reached.

Guidelines for Acts of Hospitality

Notice some simple guidelines for conducting acts of kindness in the community.

1. When Appropriate, Always Ask Permission

Unfortunately, we're aware of the litigation madness in our society today. Therefore, I recommend that your teams seek permission when performing a random act of kindness in the community. For instance, when some of our teams provide hot coffee and cocoa to shoppers at a local grocery store, we make sure that the store manager knows our intentions and has approved our being there. A philosophy to apply is "better safe than sorry." Perhaps you have heard people say, "It's easier to get forgiveness than it is to get permission." That may be true, but it's not courteous or professional. Most retailers in shopping centers and malls are more than willing to work with churches, especially when it benefits their business.

2. If Possible, Have All Your Supplies in Advance

Depending on the type of project, make sure you have plenty of supplies on hand. If the project is a big event, it is wise to have someone assigned as the leader or coordinator. This person can delegate responsibilities, arrange time schedules, get permission, and perform other tasks as needed to make the event a success. If you run out of supplies, the coordinator can either replenish the supplies or assign someone else to perform that task. Also, use *quality* equipment and products when performing community services. The people you're serving will feel valued if you use high-quality products.

3. Stick to Your Assigned Schedule and Time Arrangements

If you plan to perform a project from 9:00 a.m. until 12:00 noon, make sure you honor those time arrangements. This respects the time of both your team members and the people who may be providing you a location or space to perform your services. Time is a precious commodity in our society. Therefore, honor people's time with proficient scheduling and arrangements. The idea is to go out long enough to accomplish significant ministry while completing your project before it becomes tiresome or boring. A sufficient time span for most projects is three to four hours maximum.

4. Practice Safety at All Times

When you are performing a community project, make sure safety measures are considered. Provide bright-colored safety vests when conducting services close to a busy street. Never send teens or children out to perform tasks without proper adult supervision. Have plenty of men present when performing community acts. Have team members wear name tags or perhaps a T-shirt that promotes who and what you represent. Finally, if your community event is on a large scale, use cell phones or walkie-talkies so team members can communicate effectively.

5. Demonstrate Kindness in Attitude

The acts of kindness you perform make an incredible impression on those you serve—but only if you do it with the right spirit. If you perform an act of kindness with a disgruntled spirit, chances are you have failed to truly minister to someone. Why? Often it is not necessarily the deed that impresses but the attitude of the one performing the deed. For instance, if you are giftwrapping a Christmas gift for someone, and all you can do is complain that your feet hurt, or that there are too many "cheap" people wanting "free" giftwrapping, then you've lost your effectiveness. The whole idea of an act of "kindness" is that it is done with a spirit of humility and graciousness. Never be overbearing or rude to someone you are serving. Undoubtedly you will perform a task for someone who is ungrateful or dissatisfied in return. When this occurs, always smile and be overly courteous. Remember that a smile and a gentle voice are powerful tools to apply when dealing with mean or unsatisfied people. Don't forget: The *task* you perform is only a *tool* you use to *touch* a soul for Jesus.

6. Always Do Your Very Best

Whatever task you perform, do it to the best of your abilities. People notice laziness, apathy, and indifference. God desires our very best, and so do those we're trying to reach. This doesn't mean you have to be a perfectionist. However, performing a reasonably good job is within the limits of everyone. Your public effort will reflect either positively or negatively on your church. If your work is performed with quality, people will likely have a more positive opinion about your church. However, if your work performance is below par, people will draw the conclusion that your church must possess the same disposition (see Phil. 2:14–15).

7. Review the Pros and Cons of Every Event

The time you spend reviewing what worked and what didn't will be energy well spent. The purpose for this review is to learn how to give away God's love to the lost more effectively. Discovering what people respond to can make all the difference in an effective project. Record your findings and give this information to your pastor/REACH Team coordinator.

8. Be in a Spirit of Prayer

Intercession is important when you are performing acts of kindness. First, pray for opportunities to share your faith and bear good fruit. Second, pray as you perform the act of kindness. Being in a spirit of prayer will enhance your heart and attitude while you attempt to serve others. When it is all over, they may forget you, but pray that they will not forget the Jesus they have seen in you. Third, pray for the people you are trying to reach. Ask God to give them a pliable heart and spirit. Finally, pray for results after the project is completed. You have planted seeds; now pray that those seeds fall on fertile soil.

9. Don't Be Concerned with Seeing Immediate Results

Most people will be grateful for the service you have provided. However, don't expect to see every person you reach in church the following Sunday morning. That won't happen. God will, however, honor your efforts. I love what Paul told the churches of Galatia: "Let us not become weary in doing good, for at the proper time we will reap a harvest if we do not give up" (Gal. 6:9). Several of our REACH Teams provided acts of hospitality for a summer baseball league program. Several months later, when my son tried out for a community basketball league, his coach asked me what I did for a living. I told him I was a pastor of Fall Creek Baptist Church. He immediately said, "I know your church. You're the ones who helped in the summer baseball league with the concession stand, right?" "Wow, I can't believe you remember that," I replied. The coach then said, "Ever since we saw what you folks did, my family and I have been thinking about attending your church." His family did come and worship with our church and eventually united with our fellowship! The process took almost one year. You have to be patient for the harvest.

10. Please Do Not Charge a Fee for Your Services

Charging a fee only minimizes your effectiveness. Inevitably people will want to show their gratitude for your services by offering to pay. Don't argue with them; instead, kindly let them know that your actions are not intended for monetary gain. Share with them that your gift is the privilege of serving them with no strings attached.

11. Plan for Appropriate Expenses

Most of your community ministry projects will call for some financial support. Initially, when starting the REACH Team ministry, church funding may be limited. Therefore, I suggest that each team be willing to make financial contributions when needs arise. If your ministry project is more costly than what your team can provide, join forces with another team and pool your resources.

12. Have an Alternate Project in Reserve in Case of Inclement Weather

Because many of the community projects you perform will be outside, you need to prepare for times when the weather is uncooperative. Your attitude at such times should be positive—the attitude that bad weather just means that you will attempt to meet people's needs in a slightly different way than planned. For instance, if you planned a carwash at a local grocery store parking lot and it begins to rain, provide an umbrella escort service for patrons entering and leaving the store instead. Also, print some "free carwash coupons" (with an alternative date for the carwash) and give them to patrons as they leave the store. Remember: If you sought permission from someone for your original plan, be sure to notify them of any changes in your activity's time or location.

13. Discover What Community Projects Work Best for Your Team

It is important that your team feels a sense of ownership in whatever community project it chooses to undertake. Therefore, discover what works best for your team. In doing so, remember that people's needs differ greatly from one community to the next. What may be successful in one community may be a total flop in another. Learn the basic demographics of your local area. Determine from the demographics what specific needs exist in your targeted area.

14. As Pastors and Staff Leaders, Give Your Teams Permission to Minister Freely

Pastors do a good job teaching their flock the importance of ministry, however, some pastors tend to keep people focused only on what they deem as necessary ministries, especially when it comes to performing acts of service. As a result, church members may wait for the pastor or professional staff to lead the way instead of taking the initiative to move forward in service. Most pastors would not object to having their parishioners perform acts of service as long as it was their pastor's idea. Pastors and staff members, allow for freedom and spontaneity within your teams without always requiring permission before they embark on community projects.

15. Don't Let the Fear of Mistakes Keep You from Serving

God specializes in taking weak instruments and using them to get the glory (see 1 Cor. 1:26–31). God blesses our actions and obedience, even when we think we have failed according to human expectations. Don't let the fear of failure keep you from going out and touching lives with the love of Jesus Christ.

6

The Role of the Pastor
in Effective Leading
and Training

The pastor is the catalyst to the overall success of any outreach program. His input, involvement, and example are paramount. Unfortunately, many pastors are expected to either attend or at least verbally support every ministry activity in the church. He becomes the designated "cheerleader" for every ministry. His desire as a pastor is to see every ministry that is Christ honoring and kingdom building succeed. However, there is only so much of him to go around. Unfortunately, many pastors become so spread out and divided among ministry activities that they are rendered ineffective.

The pressure to measure up to what every church member expects is overwhelming. The sad reality is that most pastors, in an attempt to be all things to all people, eventually suffer from what I call "personal identity crisis." In other words, they lose focus on who they are, and more importantly, who God has created and called them to be. As a result, the pastor who attempts to live up to all such expectations risks his health, personal testimony, family, and overall effectiveness. Taking this a step further, Joseph Aldrich notes:

> A large percentage of pastors are discouraged and in many cases defeated. Usually they won't show it, but it's there. Working with a volunteer staff and Sunday Christians is tough. Believers' lack of commitment to Christ and His purposes crushes many of them. Scores leave the pastorate every month because their dream of shepherding a flock of God's people towards maturity turned into a nightmare.[1]

The key for a pastor who runs the risk of a "personal identity crisis" is to prioritize his primary role in the church. Naturally we would expect any pastor to model the biblical role and expectations depicted in 1 Timothy 3 and Titus. This brings us to a question: "Is the pastor to be a servant or a leader?" The answer is not either/or but both/and. He is called to be the undershepherd of the people before Christ and to serve the people on behalf of Christ. The members of the local church are called to submit and follow the godly leadership of the pastor who is called by God. While the pastor is not to be autocratic, capricious, or dictatorial, he has the designation of shepherd/overseer of the flock.

I am a firm believer that every pastor should specialize in his strengths and not spend excessive time in his weaknesses. When a pastor spends too much time in his weaker areas, his strengths suffer. There are, however, three primary areas where every pastor should focus his energy on a daily basis, while in the process, continuing to develop and display his unique God-given gifts and abilities. Those areas are *preaching/teaching*, *prayer*, and *evangelism*. Preaching/teaching and prayer stem from the imperative placed upon these disciplines as recorded in Acts 6:1–4. In the early church, the apostles sought help in the daily distribution of food among the Grecian Jews so they could focus their attention on the Word of God and prayer. It wasn't that they desired to neglect others intentionally. However, their greater God-given focus was on the Word of God and prayer. The ministry of evangelism is important because of the greatest commandment and the Great Commission of our Lord Jesus Christ (see Matt. 22:37–39; 28:19–20). Every believer is called to love God, love others, and share the gospel with others.

We see in these three primary areas (preaching/teaching, prayer, and evangelism) the twofold perspective of the church as the body of Christ. First, it is the body of Christ *gathered*. Second, it is the body of Christ *scattered*.[2] The church gathers for worship, prayer, edification, and the proclamation of the Word. But if gathering is all the church does, it defeats the mission and mandate of Jesus. Therefore, the church scatters abroad as a constant reminder to this world that God is at work in the lives of his people. Another way of expressing these three priorities of a pastor and church is found in Darrell Robinson's book, *Total Church Life*:

> The church gathers for strengthening, scatters for service. The church gathers for worship, scatters for witness. The church gathers in praise, scatters in power. The church gathers in fellowship, scatters in faith following its Lord. The church gathers to equip the saints, scatters to evangelize the sinner. . . . This is the function of the church, to exalt the Savior [worship/prayer], to equip the saints [study/proclamation of the Word], and to evangelize the sinner [evangelism]. . . . A church cannot do one of these without doing all three. If, indeed, it is doing one of them, it will be doing all three.[3]

The pastor, more than any other individual, determines the character and direction of a church. The focus on and attention to evangelism by the church is dictated by the pastor's vision (or lack thereof). Jesus's mission today is done through the church, which is led and empowered by the Spirit and shepherded by the pastor. Jesus's impact and mission is linked to and in a sense limited to the vision, obedience, and leadership of the pastor. If the pastor draws limits on the church's evangelistic efforts, it becomes limited in its outreach. If the pastor's heart lacks compassion for the lost, the church will lack that sense of compassion and urgency for the lost. The pastor is God's instrument, under the guidance of the Holy Spirit, to the church to liberate people for ministry and service and help motivate them to reach out to a lost and dying world.

Rationalizations for Not Implementing a Plan

In our day, pastors frequently offer rationalizations for not implementing a comprehensive plan of evangelism. Numerous examples of such frequently used excuses are listed below.[4]

Global Missions Should Be Our First Priority

Many pastors and churches hold to the idea that the U.S. population has been saturated with the gospel message, whereas people in other countries have experienced limited exposure to the gospel. Therefore, many of these churches designate greater amounts of funding and personal attention to global missions than to local or regional missions. I agree wholeheartedly that the local church should embrace a vision for the world harvest, however, its commitment to the world scene must be balanced by a commitment to carry out the Great Commission to those in its immediate area. In essence, they have reversed the order for which Jesus issued our mission/evangelism endeavor: "Jerusalem [local], Judea and Samaria [regional], and to the ends of the earth [global]."

I'm Called to Equip the Saints

The rationale here is that many pastors believe that their sole priority is edifying and educating the saints. They see the pulpit or the classroom as their primary mission field. I would not question the fact that there is an enormous need for biblical knowledge in the local church. In many ways, I fear that while we live in a world that offers more tools for training in theology than ever before, we find ourselves in a position of great biblical illiteracy, especially in the church. We need to edify and grow the saints. Jesus did not omit this important task when offering the Great Commission. In fact, he said specifically, "Go and make disciples [learners] of all nations . . . teaching [educating] them to obey everything I have commanded you" (Matt. 28:19–20, brackets mine). Making disciples includes winning people to Jesus and leading them to follow Christ. Paul felt it necessary to instruct Timothy, "Do the work of an evangelist" (2 Tim. 4:5). Notice that there was no argument as to whether or not evangelism was designated to him as presented in Ephesians 4:11. Paul offers the basic assumption that it was a *natural expectation* for Timothy to fulfill. Why? Timothy was the pastor of the church. He could not ask of his people what he was unwilling to do himself.

No One Possesses the Gift of Evangelism in Our Church

There has been some discussion in evangelical circles concerning evangelism as a spiritual gift. While the New Testament clearly defines the office or labor of an evangelist (see Acts 21:8; Eph. 4:11; and 2 Tim. 4:5), nowhere is there any scriptural indication relating to a specific gift of evangelism.[5] The gift is the gift of the evangelist (see Eph. 4:11). The commission to fulfill the evangelization of the world is issued corporately, not individually. Unfortunately, many in our churches do not see it this way. For too long the laity of our churches have been attending meetings, giving money, and praying, while depending on a select few (those with the gift of evangelism) to do all the witnessing. According to one survey, it takes one thousand laypersons and six ministers one year to win one person to Jesus.[6] It is a travesty to think that 95 percent of the Christians today have never lead a soul to faith in Christ. This trend must be reversed if the church is to impact our society with the gospel.

A Visible Witness Is Enough to Relay the Message of the Gospel

Some pastors and churches use the rationale that if we live godly lives before our neighbors and friends, they will see Jesus in us and automatically be drawn to Christ. There are some errors to this logic. First, there are scores of people in the world who live socially and morally astute lives but are not Christians. These people choose to live by the "golden rule," a moral code of conduct, or simply to obey the law of the land. Unfortunately, they have yet to discover that all humanity is sinful and separated from God (see Isa. 64:6; Rom. 3:10–12). A second fallacy to this logic is that a Christian is incapable of living an undefiled life. Eventually, no matter how righteous you try to live, your family, friends, and neighbors will experience your flaws and failures. Third, let's say, hypothetically, that you *were* able to live a seemingly spotless life. That does not guarantee that your neighbor will be drawn to Christ solely by your lifestyle. They may interpret your behavior as nothing more than the result of good upbringing or strict obedience to the governing laws of the land.

God's grace is not a license to sin. We should live lives worthy of the example of Jesus. However, the disposition of Jesus's life wasn't the sole means of challenging people concerning their sin. His spoken word was the instrument of conviction upon their hearts. Jesus told the righteous Nicodemus, a Pharisee and member of the Jewish ruling council, "you must be born again" (John 3:7). Nicodemus was a pillar in the community. He obeyed the law, followed the moral code of conduct, and even sought to demonstrate the religious piety of his Jewish heritage. Jesus could have easily commended him on his outstanding behavior. Instead, Jesus confronted him about his sin. It ought to be the goal of every Christian to strive toward the high calling of Jesus Christ (Phil. 3:14), and to live a life that is absent of embarrassment or shame. However, our visible testimony, though truly having an impact on our world, must never substitute for the need to verbalize the message of truth to our lost world.

God's Elect Are Chosen Already

This rationale is offered primarily on theological grounds and has proven to be more damaging than imagined. To the Christian who holds such a view of election, his argument might be: "Since God has already elected (saved) those who are to be Christians, what we say or do will have no effect on whether or not people come to Christ. If they are part of the elect, nothing can keep them from being saved. If they're not part of the elect, there's no chance for them anyway." This mind-set brings into sharp focus the difficult problem of divine election versus human free will, a problem for which we have no absolute answers this side of glory.

Substantial arguments can be made for both opinions. For instance, one cannot refute the sovereignty of God. He is and always will be the great Almighty. To say that God doesn't know who will ultimately become one of his children denies the very power and authority God claims for himself and has attested to in Scripture. Furthermore, one cannot argue that God is the one who initiates salvation (see John 1:12–13; 6:37, 44). On the other hand, if God chooses who will be saved, that would substantiate the fact God must also choose who will be sentenced to hell. That leaves us with the question, "Would a loving God intentionally create a person with no prospect of eternal life in heaven?" Nowhere are we taught that God predestines people to be eternally condemned. In fact, the Scriptures reveal that God is patient and desires that no one should perish (2 Peter 3:9).

Implementing a Plan of Evangelism

As the pastor or church leader, your role in your church's evangelism efforts is crucial. I want to address this responsibility from two perspectives: personal and corporate.

Personal Involvement

1. *Live the gospel every day.* By this I mean that it ought to be your personal goal each week to share the gospel with someone and see that person come to faith in Jesus Christ. Try winning someone to Christ who is outside your comfort zone or circle of influence. Have you ever noticed that every evangelist that comes to your church has a story about witnessing to a complete stranger while traveling on an airplane? I say this not to be flippant but rather to make a point that most of these people practice what they preach. A true evangelist's heart is bent toward lost souls. Because as pastors we are to "do the work of an evangelist," we need to reach out beyond our comfort zones and share the gospel with people we don't know.

2. *Stay close to the action.* As pastor, you need to be the primary leader of your outreach/evangelism program. It is not to say that if you pastor a large (mega) church, you shouldn't have a designated staff person directing the program. What I'm talking about is your personal involvement and visibility in the effort. People need to see their pastor winning others to Jesus Christ. They need to see their pastor making visits to the unchurched, cultivating relationships with the unsaved, and establishing contacts with the lost. You need to be seen on the front lines of evangelism in your church.

3. *Maintain your circle of influence.* Every pastor ought to keep a personal circle of influence. I started doing this a few years ago, and I can honestly say I am never at a loss of having someone with whom to share my faith. God will do the same for you if you will be obedient and faithful to this task.

4. Pray daily for souls to be saved. Every pastor ought to be a prayer warrior, especially when it comes to praying for the harvest. Amazingly, when the laity in your church sees your prayerful spirit for the harvest, many of them too will mimic that same passion for souls! As pastors and church leaders, we need to be reminded of men like Martin Luther, John Wesley, David Brainerd, George Fox, Adoniram Judson, and John Hyde. Luther said, "I have so much business I cannot get on without spending three hours in prayer." Wesley declared, "God does nothing but in answer to prayer." Brainerd wrote in his journal, "I love to be alone in my cottage, where I can spend much time in prayer." William Penn said of Fox, "Above all he excelled in prayer. The most awful, living, reverent frame I ever felt or beheld, I must say was his in prayer." Judson withdrew from business and company seven times a day for the purpose of prayer. Hyde was so characterized by prayer that he was nicknamed "Praying Hyde." It is no small wonder that these prayer warriors wielded unusual power and supernatural influence for the kingdom of God.[7]

5. Respond to cries for help. As the church grows and its ministry becomes more specialized, the pastor may not be able to be involved in the lives of every single convert. But to fulfill our call to ministry and to be like the Lord who called us, we must personally answer enough of those cries for help that we get our hands dirty and our hearts broken by hurting people. If you have decided to become a church CEO, you may never experience the soul-shaping, spiritual adventure of touching lives for the kingdom. Be sensitive to benevolent needs that come your way. Be on guard the next time you conduct a funeral service and a distant family member of the deceased is in attendance at the funeral, having never heard the gospel. Be aware of hospital visits where the opportunity to share with doctors, nurses, and attendants is abundant and often timely.

Corporate Involvement

Second, let's look at the pastor's corporate involvement in evangelism. A church and its leaders have a responsibility to God to involve its great army of laity in witness for Jesus. Four basic keys are necessary for proper implementation of a good evangelism program.[8]

1. Enlighten the church. Many Christians fail to witness because they are not educated or challenged on the subject. I urge you to preach on the subject of soul winning, challenging your flock about the biblical mandate to share their faith. Witnessing is not an option; it is a mandate for every Christian. Pastors should keep their flock accountable before God concerning the commission every Christian has received from God.

2. Enlist the church. We enlist people for practically everything under the sun. Unfortunately, one of the areas we often overlook is the ministry of evangelism. Evangelism must be given priority as a major emphasis of the church. If not, laity will be enlisted in so many committees, social functions, and recreational activities that they will have no time to commit to outreach.

3. Equip the church. Most laypeople have a deep desire to win others to Christ; unfortunately, most of them simply do not know how. This is where REACH Team comes in. REACH Team is more than learning a clever evangelistic outline or presentation. It is working with a team of Christians to develop meaningful relationships with lost people through acts of hospitality and grace. The pastor needs to be the primary person who leads in the equipping of the saints. As the pastor makes it a priority not to only share his faith but also to equip his flock, he will reap greater benefits from both his example and training of others.

4. Engage the church. Every church has a corporate witness to its local community. Unfortunately, many churches have lost their influence in their community as a result of infighting, lovelessness, or a church split. The church must seek to keep its witness strong and vibrant in the community. Therefore, as pastors, you must engage your flock to go out into the community and share their faith with everyone who is in their personal circle of influence. Just as a general sends his army out to do battle, likewise, our great commander Jesus Christ has commissioned his army to go out and engage the lost. Pastors serve as field generals who lead and engage others. Therefore, lead by example and challenge others to do the same.

7

New Beginnings
to Some Old Endings

I love the title of the book *How to Be a Contagious Christian* by Bill Hybels and Mark Mittelburg. I think all Christians ought to desire to be "contagious" when it comes to their witness. In essence, our lives should spread like a life-changing virus by infecting an already dying world with God's supernatural love and grace. The apostle Paul possessed that type of contagious and infectious spirit. He had an urgency to proclaim the message of Jesus Christ wherever he went and to whomever he came in contact with (Rom. 1:14–15). My desire is to create urgency in your heart for a new beginning in personal evangelism. Many well-meaning Christians will read a book on evangelism and agree with it in principle but do nothing about it in practice. In other words, it's the same old ending to a never-ending process. We know what we need to do, but we often fail when it comes to actually fulfilling the task required.

Practically all of us can attest to the fact that our practical application of biblical truths and precepts suffers from flaws and shortcomings. Rather than being an effervescent, infectious witness for Jesus Christ, we often find ourselves prone to being spiritually lukewarm, if not dead and dried up spiritually. Our lack of commitment results in a failure to present Christ to our unchurched friends. How, then, can we take the outward desire of sharing our faith and make it a clearly defined inward focus for our life? Allow me to share some truths and challenges that I pray will serve to motivate and inspire you to become the witness God desires you to be.

You Are Never Alone When You Witness for Christ

Thankfully we do not have to evangelize the world in our own strength. We do so on the basis of God's power. Solely on the basis of God's divine presence in us and his ability to work through us are we able to influence the lives of unbelievers we encounter. As each of us seeks to obey God's mandate to share the Good News, we cannot help but be awestruck by some of his daunting promises. For instance, Jesus said that if we witness on his behalf, the world will hate us for it. Also, if we choose to commit our lives to Jesus, Satan will seek to destroy our testimony and witness. But on the flip side rests an array of promises God has made to us representing his enduring source of empowerment and force. The greatest of these promises is found in Matthew 28:20, where Jesus says to each disciple, "And surely I am with you always, to the very end of the age."

Be mindful of these three principles that relate to the work of the Holy Spirit in the witnessing encounter. First, God uses the activity of the Holy Spirit through the Word of God. The Word of God is active and alive. It is powerful. Like a "two-edged sword," it penetrates, separates, and divides. Second, God uses the ministry of the Holy Spirit through the witness of the believer. God uses people to reach people. People are not reached in a vacuum apart from the witness of God's people. Christians sow, and God reaps (1 Cor. 3:6). Third, God uses the ministry of the Holy Spirit to bring enlightenment and conviction to the life of the unbeliever. The Bible says that the unsaved are spiritually blind to the things of God (John 12:40; 2 Cor. 4:4). The natural man cannot understand the things of God. He is in darkness (1 Cor. 2:14). Therefore, the unbeliever needs the enlightenment and conviction of the Holy Spirit.

God Calls Each of Us to Be His Witnesses, Including You

One of Satan's greatest ploys is to try to convince us that we are unworthy of serving the Lord. Satan tries to persuade us to believe that we are incapable of leaving our frailties long enough to lead others to the presence of God. This is pure deceit on the part of the devil. Fact is, every believer is frail. In our humanity none of us are worthy to stand before the Lord, much less represent him as ambassadors. What we must remember is that we are like "jars of clay." Paul said it this way, "But we have this treasure in jars of clay to show that this all-surpassing power is from God and not from us" (2 Cor. 4:7). The following story conveys this idea:

> A water bearer in China had two large pots, each hung on the end of a pole that he carried across his neck. One of the pots had a crack in it, while the other pot was perfect and always delivered a full portion of water. At the end of a long walk from the stream to the house, the cracked pot arrived only half full.
> For a full two years this went on daily, with the bearer delivering only one and a half pots full of water to his house. Of course, the perfect pot was proud of its accomplishments, perfect for which it was made. But the poor cracked pot was ashamed of its own imperfection, and miserable that it

was able to accomplish only half of what it had been made to do.

After two years of what it perceived to be a bitter failure, it spoke to the water bearer one day by the stream. "I am ashamed of myself, and because this crack is in my side, it causes water to leak out all the way to your house."

The bearer said to the cracked pot, "Did you notice that there were flowers only on your side of the path, but not on the other pot's side? That's because I have always known about your flaw, and I planted flower seeds on your side of the path. Every day when we walk back to my house, you've watered them. For two years I have been able to pick these beautiful flowers to decorate my table. Without you being just the way you are, there would not be this beauty to grace my house."[1]

Each of us has our own flaws, cracks, and imperfections. We're all cracked pots. But our cracks and flaws make our lives together so interesting and rewarding. The measure of your testimony is not based upon your accomplishments or achievements but on what God has done in and through you. We are made perfect through our weaknesses. Often the failures of our lives speak the loudest of God's immeasurable love. God is capable of providing all the resources we need to complete the task he has called us to do (Phil. 1:6).

Always Exhibit the Love of God, Especially to Those Who Are Captives of This Fallen World

We must be careful to avoid two extremes when sharing the love and grace of God to our postmodern world. The first extreme is *judgmentalism*. If we were to handpick those whom we thought truly deserved to enter into the gates of heaven, we might be hard-pressed to find any candidates. We must remember that our job is not to judge others or qualify them by our self-proposed criteria. This was the ugly attitude that characterized the scribes and Pharisees. Jesus was so sickened by their self-proclaimed righteousness and their eagerness to equate themselves as better than others that he referred to them as "hypocrites," "snakes," and "vipers" (Matt. 23:1–36). I discovered this prayer and thought how true it was for many of us.

> Heavenly Father, Help us remember that the jerk who cut us off in traffic last night is a single mother who worked nine hours that day and was rushing home to cook dinner, help with homework, do the laundry, and spend a few precious moments with her children.
>
> Help us to remember that the pierced, tattooed, disinterested young man who can't make change correctly is a worried nineteen-year-old college student, balancing his apprehension over final exams with his fear of not getting his student loans for next semester.
>
> Remind us, O Lord, that the scary looking bum, begging for money in the same spot every day (who really ought to get a job!) is a slave to addictions that we can only imagine in our worst nightmares.
>
> Help us to remember that the old couple walking annoyingly slow through the store aisles and blocking our shopping progress is savoring this moment, knowing that, based on the biopsy report she got back last week, this will be the last year that they go shopping together.
>
> Heavenly Father, remind us each day that, of all the gifts you give us, the greatest gift is love. It is not enough to share that love with those we hold dear. Open our hearts not to just those that are close to us, but to all humanity. Let us be slow to judge and quick to forgive; show patience, empathy and love.[2]

The other extreme is what I call *unrestricted consumerism*. Think about it: here in America, we live in a consumer driven society where the key to successful merchandising is to cater to the wants of the patron. This mind-set has invaded the Christian world. Today's slick marketing approach advertises time-sensitive, upbeat, non-guilt-driven devotional sermonettes, music that everybody likes (where, oh, where is this church?), flip-flops and halter tops, and by all means, nothing too judgmental, controversial, or confrontational. John MacArthur is right when he writes:

> It's Christianity for consumers: Christianity Lite, the redirection, watering down, and misinterpretation of the biblical gospel in an attempt to make it more palatable and popular. It tastes great going down and settles light. It seems to salve your feelings and scratch your itch; it's custom tailored to your preferences. But that lightness will never fill you up with the true, saving gospel of Jesus Christ, because it is designed by man and not God, and it is hollow and worthless. In fact, it's worse than worthless, because people who hear the message of Christianity Lite think they're hearing the gospel—think they're being rescued from eternal judgment—when it fact, they're being tragically misled.[3]

Both of these extremes should be avoided at all cost. We must love the lost, regardless of their condition. However, we make a grave mistake when we call people to make a mediocre commitment to Christ and his church. Love people; but love them enough to set forth the proper biblical and spiritual guidelines that God's Word outlines.

The Unchurched Are Waiting for You and Your Team to Reach Out to Them

A recent survey conducted by the Rainer Group revealed that 82 percent of the unchurched are at least somewhat likely to attend church if they are invited.[4] To put it another way, eight out of ten unchurched persons said that they would come to church if invited. This is an astonishing statistic considering the fact that there are between 160 million and 190 million unchurched people in America.[5] If so many are willing to respond to an invitation to attend church, why are so many staying away from the church?

Perhaps the answer lies with the ones who are supposed to be doing the inviting. Rainer writes, "Only 21 percent of active churchgoers invite anyone to church in the course of a year. But only 2 percent of church members invite an unchurched person to church."[6] I write this not to be critical or chastening but to challenge every reader to ask, "When was the last time I invited a nonbeliever to church?" I'm afraid that the sad reality is few Christians ever invite anyone, especially unsaved people, to church. Think about the unlimited number of opportunities you have to befriend an unchurched person. Most Christians are simply content within themselves to commit the sin of silence without any reservation. This is the greatest indictment against the twenty-first-century church.

The following truth contains a frightening prospect for every true believer. It contains the kind of inference from which, if we followed our instincts, we would tuck tail and run. Serious thought of the possibility of such a reality is almost enough to overwhelm even the strongest of believers. What reality am I referring to? *The cold reality of unbelievers' blood upon our hands.*

Out of the imagery of the Old Testament book of Ezekiel comes the idea of this modern-day reality. All major cities in the Old Testament world had a watchman stationed atop a tall tower on the wall, where a maximum range of visibility would be his. If an enemy army approached the city, the watchman's duty was to warn the city of an impending attack. However, if the watchman failed in his duty, and the city was overrun and captured, the watchman was held accountable. In other words, the blood of those massacred would be on his hands (Ezek. 33:7–9).

Some may argue that this is an Old Testament passage, therefore, it holds little relevance to the New Testament church. With the attitude of "what happened before Christ does not pertain to us," much of contemporary Christianity would reject this principle based upon irrelevancy. This mindset might be true if not for the words of Paul to the church at Ephesus. Paul, inspired by the Holy Spirit, contends that the principle of bloodguilt for negligence is still applicable in the Christian age. When he departed from the city of Ephesus, Paul boldly stated, "Therefore, I declare to you today that I am innocent of the blood of all men. For I have not hesitated to proclaim to you the whole will of God" (Acts 20:26–27). According to the New Testament, a failure to discharge the God-ordained responsibility of speaking out to unbelievers means the blood of eternal souls on our hands. The bloodguilt principle described in the Old Testament is repeated in the New Testament. This recurrence enforces its ratification in your life and mine.

Relevance suggests reality, and there is no more frightening reality in the life of a believer than the reality of being held responsible for the souls of others. That we, by our negligence, can be guilty of a kind of "spiritual homicide"—our hands being stained by the blood of lost souls because of our indifference toward those who are unsaved. What a tragic reality! This truth is a rebuke against anything short of total commitment to the task of sharing our faith, a reproof to anything short of our lives being completely controlled by the power and presence of the Holy Spirit. The reality of bloodguilt is a censure on careless living, sin-obstructed lives, and Spirit-grieving habits that often characterize the lives of Christians. This bloodguilt is a constant rebuttal to the kind of cowering fear that causes Christians to shut up when they ought to speak out.

Be Cautious of Personal Apathy, Complacency, and Indifference

I am absolutely convinced that the greatest killer of churches in our world today is the apathy, complacency, and indifference among believers toward the unsaved. Most Christians are inconsistent in their concern for the lost. Granted, sometimes we are on fire, but most of the time we are smoking embers. Our concern is based on feelings. If we feel concerned, we are more prone to share. If we don't feel a concern, we fail to share. Our efforts in reaching the unsaved must not be regulated by our feelings but by our Lord's feeling of concern for the lost. With this in mind, allow me to ask you three questions.

First, "How is your personal relationship with the Lord?" Our love for Christ is the prerequisite of effective personal evangelism. If we love him, and our hearts are in tune with him, then his interest will be our consuming interest (John 14:21).

Second, "How is your availability to the Lord's will through his Word?" God will never lead you contrary to his Word. Too many Christians get all excited about Jesus, begin to experience the genuineness of his touch, only to waste their lives pursuing self-serving experiences, all in the name of the Lord. God's will for your life is to fulfill the greatest commandment and the Great Commission, as well as the entirety of his divine Word. If you are obedient to Scripture, you cannot help but love God and lost sinners.

Third, "How is your passion to serve the Lord?" Our reason for living ought to be nothing less than a relentless pursuit of God. When you exercise a driving pursuit for God, you will be motivated to make an impact among unbelievers around you because you will share the same passion that the Lord has of seeking and saving those who are lost.

Be a Friend First, but with the Heart of an Evangelist

Over the years parents have been taught that verbal communication is far less effective than the demonstration of personal example. Another way of saying it is, "Practice what you preach," or "Actions speak louder than words." Most of us would readily agree with this counsel. If this is the case, why are so many Christians remiss in applying this practice to their witness? We must remember that evangelism is more than a slick presentation, and a soul is more than just another notch on our gospel belt. Evangelism is people—real people with hurts, pains, and sorrows. Evangelism is for people who think they have gained all of life's possessions and for those who are completely destitute. The unchurched are seeking answers to life's questions, perplexities, and conflicts. Thom Rainer, through investigative research, estimates that sixty million people in America are searching for answers to life and spirituality, and waiting for someone to share with them these answers.[7]

What brought Jesus to this world? Wrath? Judgment? Condemnation? The Bible says, "For God did not send his son into the world to condemn the world, but to save the world through him" (John 3:17). And in the verse preceding, we see that God chose to demonstrate his love for us through his Son: "For God so loved the world that he gave his one and only Son" (John 3:16). That is what the incarnation is all about—*love*. God didn't send us a tract from heaven describing his love; he sent us a living demonstration of his love—Jesus Christ incarnate. And Jesus was a *friend* to sinners. Most unchurched people are not looking for religion or religious propaganda. They're interested in others showing them the authenticity of true spirituality. They're looking for real, meaningful, and fulfilling relationships, for people that truly care about their problems and heartaches.

I did not grow up in a Christian home. Both of my parents were alcoholics. My father was a traveling salesman and was gone most of the time. My father left us when I was nine years old. By the time I was thirteen, my mother was trying to raise three teenage boys while working two jobs. She continued her alcohol consumption. When things became too difficult for her, she took her own life. While I was not a Christian, I did believe God existed. I can remember the night my mother took her life. I was laying on my aunt's couch trying to go to sleep for the night, but sleep was the last thing on my mind. I began to cry out to God, "Why is there so much hurt and sadness in my life? Why did my father leave? Why did my mother take her life? Why, God, why?"

In an act of great mercy, I truly believe God opened doors for me to live with my aunt and uncle, Lynda and Woody Neel, faithful Christians who attended church weekly. I was not used to going to church, much less accustomed to a home life that reflected any sense of value or acceptance. My new-found guardians not only welcomed me into their home but into their lives. They loved me unconditionally, even with all of my emotional baggage. They showed me God's love, a love I had longed for. To this very day I think of them as my God-sent family because of the love they have shown me through the years.

When I went to college, I met some incredible people who also loved me unconditionally. I was not a Christian at that time, although I was truly open to the gospel. At that time I met a beautiful young lady named Patty. Four years later she would become my wife. She, along with countless others, showed me the love and tender mercies of God. As a result of their love, I gave my life to Jesus Christ as a young college student. If it weren't for the genuine, authentic, and loving people who came into my life, I probably would not be here today, much less writing a book about the importance of showing God's love through personal relationships and acts of hospitality. God has demonstrated his love to me firsthand, through the actions of countless others, helping me realize that he is real and his love is everlasting. You can have an impact on the lives of others as well, if you are willing to let God use you. Be a friend to someone today. People all around us have hurts, heartaches, and hellish conditions. They're just waiting and wanting someone to reach out to them in acceptance and love.

Practice Fishing for Souls the Way Jesus Taught His Disciples, in Teams

It was a pleasant, starlit night in the town of Capernaum. From the boat out on the water, you could still see the city, serenely silhouetted against the shimmering wonder of the evening sky. A fisherman was gazing intently into the torch-lit water around his boat when an age-old call echoed from an approaching boat. "Having any luck tonight?" "I haven't caught a thing," was the disappointed response. "Neither have we experienced any favor tonight. Perhaps we should work our way toward the harbor. Our fishing is over for the night; dawn will be upon us soon."

Two sets of brothers—James and John, along with their business partners, Simon and Andrew—were washing their nets after an exhausting night of fishing. While going through their nightly routine, they saw Jesus of Nazareth coming toward them. A large crowd followed the man from Nazareth. Jesus asked if he could occupy one of the boats. From there he sat and taught the people who eagerly gathered around. Then, when Jesus finished speaking, something almost laughable occurred. He said to Simon, "Put out into the deep water, and let down your nets for a catch." Simon had to have been surprised by the request. He had been out all night and had nothing to show for it. But Simon wasn't the type who easily disappointed others, so he honored the Master's request.

You know the rest of the story. Those fishermen caught so many fish that their boats began to sink under the enormous load. Likewise, you know that Simon was so overwhelmed by the great catch, he considered himself unworthy to be in the Master's presence. Jesus's response to Simon is as important for us today as it was for Simon and the other fishermen. Jesus said, "Don't be afraid, from now on you will catch men" (see Luke 5:1–11).

These fishermen acquired a new agenda that evening. Remarkably, so did we. We too are called to be fishers of men.

When Jesus spoke of *catching* men, this was language that Simon, Andrew, James, and John knew quite well. Today when a person talks about catching fish, we naturally think of angling (with a rod and reel and a baited hook). But Jesus was referring to *net* fishing. Why is this important? I think there are some unique correlations between net fishing and the team approach to relational evangelism.[8]

First, *net fishing is an enterprise of partners.* When Simon and Andrew's boat began to sink due to the weight of the great catch of fish, they immediately called upon their partners, James and John, to come and assist. In many ways evangelism is a partnership endeavor (see 1 Cor. 3:5–6). I can honestly say that I do not know one person I have ever had the privilege of leading to Christ who was not witnessed to by someone before me. In virtually every case, God uses a multiple of witnesses to complete his harvest.

Second, *the net fisherman fishes for a living.* My uncle, Doug Heflin, was a gifted angler fisherman. He traveled all around to fishing tournaments, competing with other anglers to catch the largest fish. All he was interested in was a trophy. To him, fishing was nothing more than a sport. On the other hand, the net fisherman needs to fish in order to sustain himself and his family. So it is with the church. The church needs the gifts God has to give her, and God has chosen to build his church with his people. As more and more converts are added to the church, its ministry and mission become more enhanced.

Finally, *the net fisherman is concerned with the keeping.* Real evangelism—the kind that seeks to meet people where they are and embraces them as more than potential converts—is concerned not only with the catch but with the keeping. We are not called to make converts but to *make disciples.* Over the years I have heard pastors and vocational evangelists almost gloat over the number of converts they have won to Christ. My question is, "Where are those converts now?" The number of converts we in evangelical circles have baited, baptized, and then abandoned is a tragic reality.

Never Forget, the Gospel Is Good News to a Fallen and Destitute World

I was preparing to go to the church office the morning of September 11, 2001, when the telephone rang. My wife's voice was frantic as she instructed me to turn on the television. I asked, "What is all the news?" "You won't believe it. I promise, you're not going to believe it." The news was the greatest single catastrophe in my lifetime, probably yours as well. I was utterly stunned as I watched the television coverage of the terrorist attacks on the World Trade Center and the Pentagon. An incredible toll in innocent human lives was taken on that horrible day.

Do you remember where you were or what you were doing when you received the news of the attack? Do you remember how you felt? Appalled? Surprised? Devastated? You probably would say, "Words cannot possibly describe how I felt when I received the news about the event." Daily we are faced with the reality of one tragic event after another. People are inundated with bad news. With all of the bad news, believers need to be mindful that we have the world's greatest news to share. That's what the gospel is—Good News. Why? Because it speaks against the troubles we face daily in our world. It is news that speaks to the fallen human condition and to the incredibly difficult situations that humanity continually faces. It is good news that speaks freedom—freedom from disaster, freedom from guilt, freedom from loneliness, freedom from pain, and freedom from death. Because Jesus Christ died on the cross of Calvary, we can receive forgiveness from our sins. Because of his death, we can experience freedom from a meaningless existence or lonely circumstances. Because of his victory over sin and death, we can experience freedom over fear, pain, even death.

Like all good news, this needs to be shared. This was the role and example of Jesus's earthly ministry:

The Spirit of the Lord is on me,
  because he has anointed me
  to preach good news to the poor.
He has sent me to proclaim freedom for the prisoners
  and recovery of sight for the blind,
to release the oppressed,
  to proclaim the year of the Lord's favor.

Luke 4:18–19

And this was the message Jesus instructed his disciples to share, for when he sent them out, they "went from village to village, preaching the gospel [Good News]" (Luke 9:6). And quoting the prophet Isaiah, Paul described all the followers of Jesus who bear these good tidings like this: "How beautiful are the feet of those who bring good news!" (Rom. 10:15).

I've often wondered why Isaiah and Paul singled out the feet of those who bring good news. Feet are not the most appealing part of the human anatomy. No wonder the task of washing feet was relegated to slaves in Old Testament times. When Jesus began to wash the feet of his disciples, Peter was appalled that the Lord would lower himself to such a mundane task. He pleaded with the Lord not to wash his feet, fearing that the act was so humiliating that it would discredit the Lord's good position as a rabbi.

Paul singles out feet because of their relationship with the term *gospel*. *Gospel* was originally used in correlation to a battle that had been won. A courier or runner carried the news of victory. In all likelihood, Isaiah's reference to beautiful feet was in regard to the Israelites' freedom from Babylonian captivity. Couriers raced from the battlefields to announce that they were free at last. Paul, thinking of Isaiah's words, envisioned Christians running to announce that freedom could be received through the shed blood of Jesus Christ. Thus the feet of the early Christians carried the Good News of salvation to a lost world. And our feet today carry the same Good News!

111

What about you? Do you realize that the eternal fate of the lost world rests in our hands? God has commissioned us, his devoted followers, to carry the Good News to a world that Jesus died for willfully, and his death was not in vain. I challenge you to be bold and steadfast, courageous and gracious, loving and authentic. Work together with your brothers and sisters in the faith, befriending the unchurched, loving and accepting them unconditionally, and bringing them into the fold of the Lord. We have the glorious privilege of showing and telling people the Good News about Jesus Christ!

PART 3

UNDERSTANDING THE STRATEGY OF REACH TEAM

8

The Prerequisite Involved

People Do Matter to God

Someone once coined the phrase "People don't care how much you know until they know how much you care." How true. The fact is, the unchurched don't care how much we know about God until they know how much we care about them. Today's church must realize that more people are won to Christ by feeling and seeing God's presence in us (the body of Christ) than by all of our apologetic arguments combined. Few people, if any, are converted to Christ on purely intellectual grounds. The sense of God's presence through the church's acts of hospitality melts the hearts of the unchurched and explodes their mental, social, and religious barriers.

Some churches, perhaps without ever realizing it, have developed a subtle yet extremely prejudiced value judgment against those who are outside the church. It's as if they decide who is and who is not valuable to the kingdom of God, reasoning that only a select few (namely, those who dress like, act like, sound like, and look like them) are truly worthy of the kingdom of God. This kind of rationale deters any real motivation for spreading the gospel message of salvation.

Jesus shows us a different approach. He treated all people as equals, regardless of their social, political, or moral standing. This point is proven vividly in John's Gospel, chapters 3 and 4. It would be difficult to find a greater contrast between two people than the contrast between Nicodemus in John 3 and the Samaritan woman in John 4. Nicodemus represented the best in the nation. He was a Jew, a teacher, a Pharisee, and a member of the Sanhedrin, the Jewish ruling council. He was considered a scholar, a man of satisfactory wealth and means, and was well-respected in town. He was the kind of person you would want to be seen with in the open market or city street.

The Samaritan woman represented the worst in the nation. She was considered a "lower-class" citizen, a half-breed Samaritan, and a person with no religious affiliation. She was uneducated, noninfluential, and one of the least respected in town. No doubt the woman was shocked to hear a Jewish man ask for a drink of water from her. The normal societal prejudices of the day prohibited public conversation between men and women, between Jews and Samaritans, and especially between strangers. A Jewish rabbi (Nicodemus referred to Jesus as a rabbi) would rather go thirsty than violate these proprieties.

Nicodemus had an influential name; her name is never mentioned. They were complete opposites in every way conceivable, except for one thing—they both were sinners, lost, and in need of a Savior. Nicodemus proves that no one can rise to such heights where salvation is not required, while the woman is an example of the truth that no one can sink so low that they cannot be redeemed. Jesus reached out equally to both without prejudice or premeditated value judgments. It is by no accident that God put these two encounters of Jesus back-to-back at the beginning of John's Gospel.

Jesus associated with tax collectors and sinners, meeting them on their own level. Tax collectors and sinners, in turn, were not slow to recognize the contrast between Christ's acceptance of them and the smug attitudes of the religious crowd. Therefore, the irreligious crowd regarded Jesus as a friend and took joy in being in his presence (see Luke 7:34). Clearly the religious crowd had not taken to heart the lesson Jesus taught them previously: "It is not the healthy who need a doctor, but the sick. I have not come to call the righteous, but sinners to repentance" (Luke 5:31–32). Even after all of this, they refused to believe that Jesus had come to the world for the very purpose of seeking and saving the lost (Luke 19:10).

As Christians it is not our prerogative to decide who is worthy of our witnessing efforts and who's void of any hope. Take, for instance, Saul, the religious zealot who set out to murder Christians and destroy the infant church. He hated all Christians and was brutal in his efforts to put an end to the Christian movement. Yet, God had other plans for Saul. Jesus met Saul on the road to Damascus and revealed to him God's divine grace and mercy. Saul was dramatically and supernaturally changed. Keep in mind that Saul had a nasty reputation. Even after his conversion experience, people in the church feared his presence and doubted the authenticity of his newfound faith.

Apparently, first-century Christians considered Saul a hopeless case; therefore, Jesus witnessed to him personally. As a result, the Christian community is still reaping the results of this dynamic Christian force named Paul. Our value judgments can be misleading. Understand this truth: If God can completely change a vindictive Christian-murderer into an authentic church leader, imagine what he can do with some of the people you know.

My son was selected to play baseball. The coach asked me if I would be interested in being one of the assistant coaches. Even though I didn't know the coach, I agreed to help as much as I could. After being around the coach for a few practices and on into the season of play, I began to notice some unusual characteristics. For instance, his speech was often slurred. Sometimes he stumbled around and occasionally lost his balance. At first I thought that he might be suffering from some physical sickness. However, I soon realized that he wasn't suffering from a physical sickness; he was an alcoholic.

My first concern was for the children. As a parent I wanted to make sure that my son, as well as the other boys, was in a safe environment. Patty and I talked about this at length, and we decided that the coach was very good with the boys and presented no initial threat to their safety or well-being. My second concern was for the coach's soul and well-being. I started, somewhat awkwardly, to make an effort to befriend him. I found out that he was a social worker and psychotherapist. One day after a ball game, I asked him, "Coach, does your family attend a church anywhere?" He quickly replied, "We're Jewish, but we haven't gone to the synagogue in several years." He told me that he and his wife had filed for divorce.

I thought to myself, *What in the world have I gotten myself into?* I immediately began to make excuse after excuse to the Lord as to why it would not be a good idea for me to witness to the coach.

The more excuses I made, however, the guiltier I felt. It was as if the Spirit of the Lord was telling me, "I know all about his problems, Scott. Right now all I want you to do is show my love to this man and let him know that amid his conflict, he truly matters to me! Can you do that?" I must admit this was not an easy task. I said, "Coach, I know you're going through a tough time. Is there anything I can do to help?" To my astonishment he replied, "Yes, there is something you can do. I know you're a minister, so would you mind praying for me from time to time?" I responded enthusiastically, "Can I pray for you? Sure, I can pray for you!"

That one expression of concern, "Is there anything I can do to help?" was the key to our growing friendship, which is now in its third year. The coach is still not a professing

Christian, but I have shared the gospel with him on different occasions and he has frequently attended our church. He has also received some needed help with his drinking problem.

God reminded me through my newfound relationship with my son's coach that people, all people, matter to God. It has been a valuable, and yes, painful, lesson to learn. I realized for the first time in my twenty-plus years of ministry that I carried some underlying prejudices toward people. I can honestly say that it wasn't directly related to one's race, color, or ethnic background. However, it was worse. I had developed a value judgment system in my mind against certain people whom I judged were not viable candidates for God's salvation. All people matter deeply to God. Therefore, it is imperative that they matter to each of us as true followers of Jesus Christ.

"Okay," you might say, "I agree that people do matter to God. But to what degree?" This is a question that must be addressed. Why? Because only when you and I realize just how *much* people mean to God will we truly be stirred to care for others and motivated to share with them the gospel message of Jesus Christ. How much does God care about people? That question is answered in John 3:16: "For God so loved the world that he gave his one and only Son, that whosoever believes in him shall not perish but have eternal life." Two words bring out the utter depth of God's compassionate care for all people. The first word is *gave*. God loved us enough that he gave something, namely, his one and only Son, Jesus Christ, as a living sacrifice for our sins. Giving gifts to others has been a part of our culture for centuries. Whether they are birthday gifts, wedding gifts, or Christmas gifts, we give gifts to others to demonstrate our love, appreciation, and concern. I've given a lot of gifts in my day, and some were quite expensive, even sacrificial according to my bank account. But none of these gifts would come close to the enormous sacrifice of giving up one of my children. I could never make such a sacrifice.

Now consider our heavenly Father. He loved us so much he was willing to give his one and only Son as a love gift for our sin. Think about it: God, Creator and Sovereign of all creation, humbled himself and became a man. But he didn't stop there. He willingly died on a cruel cross on a hillside called Calvary for us. God became a man and willfully sacrificed himself for our sin. What a gift!

The second word from John 3:16 is *perish*. It is the Greek word *apoletai*, which refers not to complete annihilation but rather a final destiny or ruin in hell apart from God, who is joy, peace, and eternal life. With a heavy heart but a clear conviction, the church must wake up to the utter and dire reality of hell. Scores of people we know and love who are without Christ are destined for eternal damnation.

Not long ago, I made a pastoral visit to a young couple who had recently come to our Sunday morning church services. The visit began with the usual small talk about family, jobs, background, and interests. As we grew comfortable with one another, I asked the young couple about their personal church background. The young man spoke up and said, "I grew up in the church. My parents took me to church since I was a baby. I was baptized in a Baptist church." He went on to say that since college days he had gotten away from the church and, now married with two children, realized the need to get back into the church setting.

I then asked the young wife about her church background. She said, "I also grew up in the church. My mother took me to church, and I have always been a member of the Mormon Church." I quickly realized that this young lady was not a Christian. I asked her a question: "Who in your opinion is Jesus Christ?" She said, "Well, I've always been told that he is a good man who loved people and helped others in need." I then asked her if I could tell her more about Jesus Christ and what the Bible says about him. She readily agreed. I told her that Jesus was God's only Son. That he was the God-Man, completely God, completely man. I told her that Jesus was born of the Virgin Mary, lived a sinless life, and completely honored and obeyed his heavenly Father. I then told her that Jesus was God's sacrificial lamb who willingly died for our sins, hers and mine, to save us from eternal punishment and hell.

I said, "Do you understand everything I have said to you at this point?" She said, "Yes, in fact, you are the first person to ever tell me that there was a real hell and that if I die without Jesus, that is where I will be forever." I told the young wife that God loved her and desired that she not go to hell. I then read to her John 3:16 and told her that with Jesus in her heart she would never perish in hell but have eternal life in heaven. I asked her, "Would you like to receive Jesus and have eternal life in heaven?" She said, "Yes, I would very much."

As I left their home that evening and reflected on the event, God reminded me of something I hope I'll never forget. That young wife didn't have the foggiest idea about hell or eternal damnation. In fact, she was headed for an eternal punishment and going to perish forever apart from God. This may not sound politically correct in our postmodern society, but the church *must* warn the unbelieving world of the eternal damnation that awaits all those outside of God's grace and forgiveness. Our postmodern world doesn't want to talk about hell. To many today, hell is nothing more than a myth, fable, or a legend. And the sad reality is that most ministers rarely, if ever, preach or speak of the reality of hell. Only when the church gets a clear picture and perspective of hell will we truly be motivated beyond our comfort zones to plead for the souls of lost people all around us.

When you begin to realize just how much God cares about you, you'll start caring more about others around you. When you realize what God has done for you—the trials and tribulations he has delivered you from, the hurts and heartaches that he has brought you through—then you begin to understand just how much you (and others) matter to him.

9

The People Involved

Anyone in the Church Can Do This Ministry

In 1996, while serving as pastor of a church in Montgomery, Alabama, I became acquainted with a dynamic pastor named John Ed Mathison, who serves as senior minister of the Frazer Memorial United Methodist Church. While Frazer Memorial started from humble beginnings, under Mathison's leadership it quickly grew to the largest average worship attendance of any congregation in the United Methodist Church. I had the opportunity one day to sit in John Ed's office and talk to him about Frazer Memorial. I asked him, "What do you think is the most significant reason for the growth here at your church?" John Ed replied, "Scott, I get asked that question several times a month. The answer is simple: It is the overwhelming involvement of our laity in every area of our church." He went on to say, "Our church continues to grow because people invite people to visit and become a part of our church. The bottom line for church growth is that God uses people to reach people. In our case, church members who find deep satisfaction in their ministry experience here at Frazer Memorial are excited and invite their friends and loved ones to worship here. As a result, people are experiencing the joy of seeing God work through them to meet the needs of others around them. It's contagious!"

I have found this to be true throughout my entire ministry. The secret of growth is the personal involvement of the church membership in meaningful ministry. Church members actively involved in a worthwhile ministry in the church are more interested in sharing what God is doing through them than finding fault and criticizing others. I've discovered that people who are busy rowing don't have the time or energy to rock the boat! People who are absorbed in serving and witnessing create a contagious atmosphere for inviting people and encouraging others to serve.

A major problem in many churches today is that many members have the mind-set that ministry is to be done by the professional clergy or ministerial staff of the church, and that laypersons are the recipients of that ministry. This attitude is killing the effectiveness of the church. In fact, I fear that if this misconception is not corrected in our churches, the results will be devastating. Even now we are dangerously close to echoing the words from the book of Judges where it declares, "After that whole generation had been gathered to their fathers, another generation grew up, who knew neither the LORD nor what he had done for Israel" (Judg. 2:10).

Much like the people who comprised the early New Testament church, we today often have difficulty with the paradox of giving and receiving in ministry. The Gospel accounts record Jesus's challenge that "Whoever finds his life will lose it, and whoever loses his life for my sake shall find it" (Matt. 10:39). The laity discovers the abundant life as they lose their lives in service.

Evangelism for the Masses

The New Testament word for "church" is *ekklesia*. It is derived from two words meaning "called out." The church is a group of people who have been called out of a worldly society into a special relationship with God and others in order to go back into that worldly society to serve and witness. First Peter 2:10 defines this clearly: "Once you were not a people, but now you are the people of God." Being called out by God naturally sets the church apart from the rest of society. In essence we are as Jesus defined us, "salt of the earth" (Matt. 5:13). When you add salt to a food product, the food doesn't look any different but the salt enhances its taste. Our significance in life evolves from God's calling in our lives for the ministry of service within his body called the church. And because we were nobody before God called us, we bring nothing to the table except his divine and immeasurable grace. We have no room to boast. We are not called because of our merit, talent, or significance. Our significance comes from the fact that God initiates the call to us and we respond with a life of surrender and service (see Eph. 2:8–10).

Perhaps the most defining picture of the New Testament church is found in Paul's first letter to the Corinthian church. In chapter 12, Paul compares the church body to the human body. Through this comparison, Paul points out the functions of the various members of the body. Each part of the body has its own individuality, yet each member discovers its overall significance in its functional relationship to the other members of the body. The individual parts of the body function together as a cohesive unit. Each individual part of the body has a specific function to perform. No one member of the body is any more or less important than another. If the physical body is without one of the functions, it is naturally incomplete. But when all parts of the body carry out their individual functionary role, the body can reach its maximum potential and capacity.

This is a beautiful illustration of what the church should be. Each member is like an individual part of the body. Each member has a ministry to perform. No one should ever consider his or her ministry more important than another's. The purpose of each individual's ministry is not for the purpose of highlighting itself but to give wholeness and cohesiveness to the entire church function. In fact, every member of the church should have a specific place and purpose for ministry involvement. Unfortunately, a lot of "handicapped churches" in our society today try to function without all their body parts.

The REACH Team ministry is designed to incorporate all the talents, gifts, and abilities of the body for outreach and evangelism. In effect the REACH Team concept opens wide the door of possibility toward liberating the laity. I believe that the evangelistic mission of the church is hindered greatly because "professional" staff assume too much responsibility for outreach, thus not allowing freedom for the laity to reach the harvest. Liberating the laity for evangelistic ministry and service can bring genuine renewal in the church. After all, nothing is more exhilarating for any believer than to lead a lost soul to faith in Jesus Christ! As a pastor, the REACH Team concept opens for me the best possibility for putting evangelism back into the hands of the laity where it biblically belongs.

When we first began REACH Team in our church, I approached a young couple in our church, Doug and Shelly Lehman, to participate in the new ministry. Shelly is the type of person who never meets a stranger. She is outgoing, enthusiastic, and bubbly. Doug is the complete opposite—quiet, reserved, and introverted. When I called Shelly to see if she and Doug would be interested in this type of ministry, Shelly immediately responded, "Yes, we would love to be a part of this effort!" Then she paused for a moment, as if to rethink her initial response, and said, "Pastor, I'm okay with this, but I don't think it is something that Doug will want to do. As you know, he gets a little fearful when it comes to talking to new people."

I encouraged her to come and bring Doug to our initial information meeting scheduled the following Sunday night. They, along with fourteen other families, attended the first organizational meeting. I shared what REACH Team was all about and how God could use anybody, regardless of their perceived limitations, to reach out to the unchurched. After the meeting I walked up to Doug and said, "Well, what do you think?" He had a nervous look about him as he answered, "Pastor, I really want to serve the church, but I don't know if I can do this or not." I asked, "Why do you feel this way?" "Because I'm not good at approaching people about their faith." I must have startled him when I immediately replied, "Doug, neither am I." "Really . . . you really mean that?" "Absolutely. In fact, it's one of the most intimidating things I do as a pastor." Doug's nervousness began to subside when I confessed that "even the preacher" gets nervous about sharing his faith.

That night I asked Doug and Shelly to serve on my REACH Team. They agreed, although Doug was somewhat hesitant to give it a try. The first thing my team did was host a cookout at my house and invite some recent guests and visitors who had attended our church. The setting was low-key. People sat around and shared small talk about families, careers, and activities. It was a great evening. After the evening was over, I asked Doug, "How was it?" He said, "Scott, this was great! I don't have any problem doing this kind of outreach. Let's do it again real soon!"

Our next team event was serving in the concession stand at a local Little League park. Several of our teams volunteered our services for the day (free of charge), and only asked for permission to hand out brochures about our church. Doug and Shelly came and worked for four hours. Doug made popcorn, hot dogs, and snow cones. He served numerous soft drinks and candy bars. For four hours he simply served the needs of others and showed them the love of Jesus Christ. In the process, he also gave away hundreds of brochures to the more than two thousand attendees that day. Again I asked Doug, "Well, what do you think about REACH Team now?" He enthusiastically replied, "This is easy, pastor. If I can do this, anybody can!"

Doug, like many other church members, is willing, able, and desirous to serve but just needs to find his niche and place of ministry. Doug discovered that winning people to the Lord doesn't always require you to step out of your comfort zone. Providing acts of hospitality to strangers, sharing a casual conversation with a new church prospect, or simply befriending a neighbor or work associate can all lead to significant encounters for showing and sharing the love of Jesus Christ.

What's Holding You Back?

When the topic of personal evangelism comes up, church members begin to look for the exit. Christians make a number of excuses as to why they cannot share their faith in Christ. These excuses vary and would fill a book by themselves. Following are some of the primary excuses Christians offer for not sharing Jesus.

Excuse #1: "I'm Not Good Enough to Share Jesus"

Many Christians convince themselves that they are simply not "good enough" to share their faith. What they mean by this is that they have been, or are presently, too sinful to be effective in sharing their faith. In some ways this is a personal guilt problem. Christians feel guilty about their sinful past or ashamed about their disobedient present and as a result convince themselves that they are not worthy to tell someone else how to come to faith in Jesus.

If you are one of these Christians, understand this: No one, especially a Christian, is perfect. Paul writes in Romans

3:23, "For all have sinned and fall short of the glory of God." And because our sinful behavior is often displayed publicly, others will see your sinfulness. I am in no way condoning or excusing sinful behavior, especially in the life of a believer. Our goal as disciples of Jesus is to follow his glorious example for our daily lives. That's why Paul reminds us: "Whatever happens, conduct yourselves in a manner worthy of the gospel of Christ" (Phil. 1:27). However, one reality that every believer must face is that at some point in our walk with Christ we will fall short of his glory. But as the old saying goes, "Don't throw the baby out with the bathwater." Realize that how we handle our failures as Christians can be the genuine essence of faith that makes a radical difference in the overall view of unbelievers around us.

One of the pitfalls for unbelievers is the fear that they cannot measure up to the Christian faith, therefore it is a futile attempt to try. Allow me to illustrate: Have you ever been shopping for a new home and decided to go into one of the model homes? The model is perfect in every measure. The landscaping is immaculate; the craftsmanship, impeccable; the interior design, breathtaking; the furnishings, gorgeous. When your tour is complete, you walk away shaking your head in awe. You convince yourself that you will never own a home like that! In fact, you wish you had never laid eyes on the house because in the back of your mind, the home you can afford will never match up to what you have just witnessed. Many unbelievers convince themselves that the church is comprised of perfect people, perfect families, and perfect marriages. They develop a mind-set that says, "I'll never be able to attain such a perfect status."

Lost people need to see that Christians aren't perfect, just forgiven. Truth be known, no one wants to be around someone who is seemingly perfect all the time. All that does is make the imperfect one feel completely inadequate and inferior. The key is transparency in our daily witness. Let your unchurched friends see your disappointments and frustrations.

Let your neighbors see the wrestling match you wage with moral dilemmas and ethical issues. And by all means, let unbelievers know that your salvation is not based upon your "good deeds" but rather on God's immeasurable grace. The unchurched need to know that Christians also get sick, lose jobs, experience hardships, have disobedient children, suffer divorces, take Prozac, and simply mess up in life. We're real people; sometimes we too are broken, wounded, angry, and disillusioned. The great English World War II leader Winston Churchill once said, "Success is going from failure to failure without a loss of enthusiasm." We all blow it from time to time. What lost people need to know is what we as believers have discovered—namely, a faith and salvation that will be there for them even when they fail.

Excuse #2: "I Don't Have the Qualifications to Share Jesus"

For the vast majority of believers, it is quite natural to feel inadequately equipped to talk about Jesus. I try to convince people that they do not need to attain a seminary degree or serve on the mission field in order to be qualified to share Jesus with a lost person. Training is important, and to a particular degree, that is what this book is all about. However, sharing your faith is actually one of the easiest things we can do in our Christian life. Think about the word *witness*. It is actually the Greek word *martys*, from where we get our English word *martyr*. We all know that a martyr is someone who is put to death for his or her belief or cause. The definition of the original word itself isn't as bad as it sounds; *martys* means to give an account or record. In the case of one sharing his or her faith, it is simply sharing what Christ has done for you.

If the great harvest of souls is going to be brought to Christ, every believer must be bold and courageous enough to bear a witness through word and deed. God is looking for faithful, transparent believers, not perfect ones. Most of us will never be at a place in our Christian faith where we feel completely qualified to share our faith. God doesn't want you to wait until you have all the answers before you share his glorious Good News. God is willing, ready, and desirous to use you right now, just the way you are in his glorified redemptive state.

One of my favorite passages of Scripture is 1 Corinthians 1:26–31. In this passage, Paul tells us that God specializes in using weak, foolish, and lowly instruments to accomplish his work. Simply stated, God has chosen to use ordinary people to do extraordinary things. Look at the twelve disciples Jesus chose—ordinary, common people. None of them came from lofty backgrounds, elevated beginnings, or elite positions. But God used them to change the world.

You don't have to have a theological degree hanging on your wall to be an effective witness for Jesus Christ. Don't allow what you perceive to be a lack of expertise keep you from being a soul winner. You may stumble, stutter, or step over your words at times, but don't give up on the opportunity to be a shining witness for the cause of Christ.

Excuse #3: "I'm Afraid to Share Jesus!"

Without question, fear is the greatest hindrance to a person sharing Jesus. I love the story told by Bill Fay in his book *Share Jesus without Fear*.

One day, I had a layover at an airport, so I went to the Red Carpet room to wait for my flight. While I was there, I saw Mohammad Ali, sitting at a table with a briefcase full of tracts about the Moslem faith. I stopped to visit, and he gave me a couple of his pamphlets. Because of his illness, Parkinson's disease, it took a long time for him to sign his name at the bottom. As I watched him, I thought, "Here is a man, giving his all with what little physical and mental abilities he has left, to share a lie. Yet too many Christians sit back, too afraid to share the truth."[1]

The fear excuse comes in many forms:

"If I talk about Jesus, I'm afraid I will mess up."

Fear of failure is a universal response. Perhaps you are thinking, "Talking about Jesus is risky business." I agree in that by the very nature of risk it involves potential of failure. What you must remember is that taking a "risk" for Jesus is actually no risk at all. What do I mean by that? Simply this: We need to remember that the outcome of talking about Jesus is not up to us. Jesus is the Lord of the harvest. You are only responsible for delivering the message, not the response. The late Dr. Bill Bright, founder of Campus Crusade for Christ, defined the art of witnessing as "taking the initiative to share Christ, in the power of the Holy Spirit, and leaving the results to God."[2] Jesus, through the convicting and converting work of the Holy Spirit, is the harvester. We are seed planters and cultivators for the harvest. When you look at witnessing from this perspective, it tends to take the pressure off, doesn't it? The only real failure about sharing your faith is the unwillingness to share at all.

"If I talk about Jesus, I'm afraid people might reject me."

Some people are afraid of the fear of rejection. (This will be addressed in detail in chap. 14.) They are afraid that if they share their faith they will be looked upon as a religious fanatic. We often remain silent in fear of what we perceive others will think about us. This may be uncomfortable to consider, but each day you choose to be silent with an unchurched friend about Jesus is another day you silently love them right into hell. Let's be honest; we are all fearful of persecution. When you come to Christ, you are never promised a "persecution-free" life. In fact, Jesus said, "Remember the words I spoke to you: 'No servant is greater than his master.' If they persecuted me, they will persecute you also" (John 15:20). But consider the greater reward of faithful obedience to the Lord: "Blessed are those who are persecuted because of righteousness, for theirs is the kingdom of heaven. . . . Rejoice and be glad, because great is your reward in heaven" (Matt. 5:10, 12).

"If I talk about Jesus, I'm afraid I will lose friendships."

Others are afraid that if they share their faith they run the risk of losing a friend. I always respond, "What kind of true friend will openly reject me if I am sincerely trying to help them with the greatest need in their life?" Yet, read what Jesus said in Luke 12:51–53: "Do you think I came to bring peace on earth? No, I tell you, but division. From now on there will be five in one family divided against each other, three against two and two against three. They will be divided, father against son and son against father, mother against daughter and daughter against mother, mother-in-law against daughter-in-law and daughter-in-law against mother-in-law." Why is it this way? Because when you choose to follow Jesus, it may cost you certain relationships. You have to be willing to die to yourself completely and leave the complete results to Christ.

Recognizing Common Sources of Fear

Fear has some common sources. First, Satan, your adversary, is a source of some of your fear. The devil is in the business of thwarting our spiritual plans, actions, and mission objectives. Perhaps his greatest work can be witnessed in the barriers of fear he erects around us. Satan knows the incredible power of the gospel. He is fully aware that every day he loses souls from his grasp because of people like you and me who share our faith willingly. Therefore his strategy is to hinder you from sharing your faith with those who need so desperately to hear.

A second contributing source of fear is the overwhelming number of people who are without faith in Jesus Christ. As we recognize the daunting task before us, we may feel overwhelmed and underequipped for the task. At this point we must remember that Jesus is Lord of the harvest; we're not. We are his appointed messengers. With this in mind, know that we are not considered "hired gunslingers" who keep notches in our belts of all the souls we have won to Christ. We should have an urgency to share because time is running short. But keep this in mind: winning the world to Jesus Christ begins with one soul at a time.

We create a third source of fear when we choose to put too much emphasis upon ourselves rather than the needs of others. We must answer this question: "Will I allow fear to control my life, or will I submit completely to Jesus Christ and allow him to cover my fears?" Like Jesus, we are called to serve others. First Peter 4:10 reminds us, "Each one should use whatever gift he has received to serve others." We all have gifts, talents, and abilities to share with others. The key is submitting completely to Jesus Christ all that he has given to us. Jesus said, "If anyone would come after me, he must deny himself and take up his cross and follow me" (Matt. 16:24). When we put Christ first in everything we do, our focus is on him rather than on ourselves.

Hundreds of excuses exist for our unwillingness to share the gospel. But face the facts: Excuses are nothing more than smoke screens we fabricate to hide our real reasons for not doing something. Don't worry about your perceived weaknesses, inadequacies, or inabilities. Remember, soul winning and sharing your faith isn't about you; it's about God and the lost soul with whom you are sharing. It's okay to be vulnerable, transparent, and human. Just be yourself, but allow the power of Jesus to shine through all of your weaknesses.

10

The Process Involved

Building Meaningful Relationships

D r. Noah Kersey, a psychologist and family therapist, once told me that one of the greatest destroyers of marriages and family relationships is the failure of spouses and family members to communicate. Conflicts and difficulties are inevitable in long-term relationships, however, the secret to building meaningful relationships is not to eliminate the potential conflicts but to address them effectively as obstacles to overcome.

The same basic principle holds true for reaching and ministering to the unchurched. We cannot possibly hope to guide the unchurched through the gospel and integrate them into the life of the church body if we do not comprehend the issues that keep them away from the church. The unchurched have personal needs and expectations regarding spirituality and church life that we as a church must meet.

And the key to fulfilling those needs is establishing meaningful relationships.

One of the keys to the overall success of REACH Team is the emphasis placed upon building meaningful relationships with the unchurched. In recent years, my conviction has been that the church has concentrated more on *entertaining* the unchurched than *embracing* the unchurched. What I mean is that the church is more concerned with providing an effective, appealing, or entertaining worship service, musical program, or special event to attract the unchurched into their church. In fact, many churches have all but abandoned any other type of outreach effort beyond that of attracting the unchurched to a worship service. Our mind-set is "Ya'll come." The problem with this attitude is that it is contrary to Scripture. Jesus was emphatic when he said, "Go therefore to every nation" (Matt. 28:19). The act of worship is paramount for the life of any believer or any church. However, pushing to get the unchurched connected with the church solely through the worship service is shortsighted at best. If we are truly serious about reaching our unchurched generation for the kingdom of God, we must multiply our efforts and increase our entry points into the church without compromising the message of the gospel.

In his book *Growing Your Church from the Outside In*, George Barna attempts to answer this question: If 95 percent of Americans believe in God, why don't they all go to church? The Barna Research Group spent over two years dialoging with many of the unchurched in our society. Barna noted that one perspective became quite clear: "The likelihood of returning to or remaining at a church largely depends upon the nature of the people in any particular congregation. Theology matters, but in the minds of the unchurched (and, quite frankly, most of the churched), the friendly and caring nature of the people matters more. . . . Slightly more than one-third of the unchurched recalled with warmth the preaching and teaching at the churches they had attended; but for most people, the intellectual and substantive emphasis was less meaningful than the emotional or relational emphasis of churches."[1] Barna goes on to offer a personal word of testimony from a former veteran of the church who had dropped out and was considering a return to the church:

> I probably wouldn't know good religious teaching from bad, or a great sermon from one that breaks every rule in the preaching manual. But I sure know nice people from jerks, and real people from hypocrites. I would stay at a church with lousy teaching but genuinely friendly people—people who got to know me and cared about me and respected my needs and boundaries—before I would stay at a place with perfect teaching and lousy people.[2]

Many within the unchurched community are searching for meaningful relationships. The problem, however, is that the average American, who either has or is in the process of fulfilling the American Dream, is lost between gaining "more things" and establishing meaningful relationships. More and more people in the marketplace are not looking for more things but authentic friendships. George Gallup Jr. has stated, "Americans are among the loneliest people in the world."[3] This seems unbelievable when you think of the billions of dollars of discretionary money that we spend each year for entertainment. If Americans have the ability to "buy" so much entertainment, how can they possibly be so lonely?

In a world of overscheduled time and fragmented lives, the church can be the primary source for the establishing of meaningful relationships. People are searching for a place to belong. In this postmodern age, the church is truly one organization that promotes the function of total community as a vital element of its overall strategy and mission. The author of Hebrews spells out this objective clearly: "Let us not give up meeting together, as some are in the habit of doing, but let us encourage one another—and all the more as you see the Day approaching" (Heb. 10:25). The early church understood that the decision to become one of Christ's disciples also included the commitment to make the church body the primary existence for their social structure, even if it meant forsaking other personal encounters.

The REACH Team ministry attempts to go beyond many "intentional" evangelistic strategies that call for visits with persons whom we know vaguely by name, or by information provided on an outreach card. REACH Team teaches the evangelizer to personalize his or her outreach efforts. Each team participant is trained in and required to develop meaningful relationships with the unchurched that come from three primary areas of identity:

1. *Prospects* Assigned to Your REACH Team

Each REACH Team will be assigned prospects who have attended their church in recent days. There are various entry points in every church; therefore, it is important to keep track of all unchurched people who make contact with your church and see to it that they are placed immediately on a REACH Team's prospect list. Remember: The vast majority of people who visit a church are looking to establish meaningful relationships and friendships. It is, therefore, extremely important that the REACH Team participants make "an initial contact" with the unchurched visitor within the first few days of their first visit to the church.

What is involved with an initial contact? I have discovered over the years that the person being visited is often quite guarded and reserved with their time. Their social schedules are packed full of engagements, appointments, and obligations. Because of this, an unannounced, cold-call visit is rarely welcome and is interpreted more as an intrusion of privacy. The REACH Team ministry suggests that a personal, handwritten note be the first avenue of contact, and should be followed up within forty-eight to seventy-two hours with a personal phone call from the REACH Team member who wrote the initial note. This process allows the prospect to be acquainted with a person by name (i.e., personal note), and a warm greeting without an unannounced intrusion. When making an initial contact, try the following suggestions:

- Welcome the prospect to your church: "We're glad you have visited with us!"
- Offer a personal invitation to the prospect to revisit the church (worship service, Bible study class, special event, and so on).
- Offer to sit with the prospect during the revisit. The unchurched often feel uncomfortable attending a new place where they have no established relationships.
- Seek more information about the prospect (i.e, "Are you new to the area? Married? Children? Occupation? Interests? Hobbies?"). However, don't make this an inquisition. Simply ask general questions that show a genuine interest in the prospect.
- Finally, ask the prospect if he or she has any needs that you or your REACH Team members can help with (i.e, locating schools, doctors, shopping centers, helping unpack, or even personal prayer concerns). The key is to demonstrate genuine concern for the prospect through your inquiry.

It is also important to maintain continual contact with your assigned prospect. Steady contact should continue until the prospect unites with your church family or chooses to no longer have contact with your church and desires no further contact by the REACH Team members. Elmer Towns states that the average church prospect needs a minimum of seven "touches" (personal contacts) by church members before he or she considers seriously joining the church fellowship.[4] Interestingly, studies reveal that churches making the most contacts tend to do the best job of attracting and bonding prospects and new members to the church.

Building meaningful relationships with assigned prospects is more than teaching someone habits of church attendance, or even correcting a behavior. Building meaningful relationships requires a total immersion into a group fellowship, group values system, and group awareness. These important and often lifelong relationships cannot be built by forced or manipulated circumstances. The relationship should develop naturally as a social process of life. Just as people can be placed together but not forced to love, prospects can be assigned to a REACH Team but not forced to engage with that group. It is a process that must be developed through genuine and authentic care and attention. Below are just a few reasons why maintaining contact with assigned prospects is vital:

- A personal relationship helps the prospect identify with the church (it offers a sense of belonging and acceptance).
- A personal relationship provides the prospect with someone with whom they can ask questions and seek answers concerning the church's ministries and programs.
- Relationships help bring the prospect into the basic activity and arena of the church; they become participants not just spectators.
- A personal relationship aids in building bridges that seek to meet the needs of a prospect (i.e., social, emotional, marital, and spiritual).

2. *Potential Prospects* You Cultivate through Your Circle of Influence

All of us have a circle of influence in our lives—people we come into contact with and with whom we have some form of relationship. These relationships may vary; nonetheless, they are all people who come in and out of our lives to some degree. Our circle of influence includes:

- family relationships (spouse, children, parents, relatives)
- close friends
- neighbors
- work/school associates
- marketplace encounters

Family Relationships

The best place to begin cultivating evangelistic relationships is within your immediate family. In an in-depth study focusing on the unchurched, Thom Rainer states, "While we would not diminish the importance of marketplace relationships for evangelism, our study of the formerly unchurched found that family member relationships were even more important. And of the different family members, wives were the ones most often mentioned as important in influencing the formerly unchurched to Christ and the church."[5] I have found this to be true over the years, especially with the wife's influence over her husband, or a mother's influence over her child.

Such is the case for Jim and Sally Fish. Sally tells a wonderful story about the influence God gave her over her husband, and how Jim ultimately came to know the Lord as his Savior.

I was saved in 1970. Our children were each saved at preteen ages. We all (except Jim) grew in our faith and love for the Lord. We never tried to "browbeat" Jim, but we didn't soft-pedal it either. Jim began attending church with us every Sunday. He rarely mentioned the sermon or the worship service—my guess is that his mind was on the Sunday afternoon ball games that followed. We prayed at every meal, even in public places. Nonetheless it was a very dark time in my life. I hung on to the Lord with both hands because it was so difficult being married to a nonbeliever. Jim went out and bought a new motorcycle. I hated it, but I sat behind him and literally prayed for him as we rode together. I was sure that God did not save me to destroy my marriage; however, it was heading down that path. Finally one day I told the Lord, "If he (Jim) is never going to love you like I love you, then please take him out of my life." Amazingly, when I took my hands off the situation, the Lord worked in a wonderful way. I had prayed for more than fourteen years for Jim to be saved. It was certainly a trying time for my entire family. But God was faithful, and prayer coupled with perseverance paid off. In 1984 Jim acknowledged faith in Jesus Christ. My prayers were answered. Our love for the Lord and for one another has grown steadily ever since that life-changing day.

Do you have a family member who is not a Christian? If so, I strongly urge you not to give up, especially if you have tried repeatedly to share your faith. Quite often, those who are the closest to us turn out to be the most resistant to our witness. Sally and her children prayed for more than fourteen years for Jim. At times it was wearisome and trying, but they never gave up on him. And as a result, Jim is a dynamic Christian who serves the Lord with all of his heart.

Close Friends

Some of our friends are actually closer to us than our immediate family members. A close friend is someone in whom we can confide. A close friend is there for you when you're in the middle of a crisis. Ask yourself, "Is my close friend saved?" "Have I ever taken the time to share with my close friend the love and grace that is found in Jesus Christ?"

Neighbors

One of the greatest untapped areas for evangelism is in our own backyard. When my family first relocated to the Indianapolis area, we lived in an apartment complex just a few miles from our church. A few days after moving in, we began meeting some of our neighbors. In the apartment right below us was a divorced man with three daughters. The father had custody of the girls a few evenings a week and every other weekend. Our children began playing with his children, and before long, we developed a relationship with our newfound neighbors. His daughters began attending our children's program. The two oldest children both made professions of faith. And it all stemmed from developing a casual relationship with a neighbor.

Think about the people who live next door to you, or right down the street. Have you taken the time to introduce yourself to them or reach out to them through some type of random act of hospitality? It's amazing how the Lord opens doors to our unchurched neighbors when we offer to check their mail or mow their lawn when they are away on vacation. Or perhaps take a meal or dessert to them when they go through a crisis event. Or offer to babysit their children and give your neighbors a night out on the town.

Work/School Associates

Numerous people come in and out of our daily lives through work and school acquaintances. I serve as an adjunct professor for Indiana Wesleyan University. Every class I teach offers an opportunity to reach out to new students by sharing my faith and inviting them to church. Think about the people you work with every day. Have you taken the time to get to know some of them? What about their spiritual condition? A glorious mission field awaits if we take the opportunity to cultivate some meaningful relationships with others we work with or go to school with each day.

Marketplace Encounters

These are the various potential relationships we all share in the mainstream of our lives. These relationships may develop with the waitress at the restaurant, the clerk at the department store, or the mechanic at the local automotive dealership. One such encounter occurred in my life a few years ago with Brenda, who worked as a manager of a local dry cleaner. Periodically I took some of my suits and dress shirts into her business for dry cleaning. We began to recognize one another and share some casual conversation. One day she said to me, "You've got to be a preacher!" I said, "How did you guess?" She said, "Well, first of all, you bring me a lot of suits to dry-clean. Second, I figured by the way you talk you must be a preacher." I took that opportunity to tell Brenda about our church and invite her to a worship service. While Brenda was already a Christian, she was not attending a local church regularly, and through our marketplace encounter, she began attending our church.

3. People I Intentionally Reach Out to through *Acts of Hospitality*

While this type of outreach is not new to the Christian community, it has not been a major factor in evangelistic outreach for most evangelical churches. Perhaps the clearest title for this type of outreach is *servant evangelism*—"demonstrating the kindness of God by offering to do some act of humble service with no strings attached."[6] Think about this: If the local church exists to serve people—not only its own members but the community in which it is located—then it must minister effectively to the needs of all people. And demonstrating acts of hospitality with *no strings attached* is a dynamic way to tell the unchurched they are cared for and loved. Something about seeing and experiencing God's love in action stirs the heart of even the most hard-hearted individual. People are naturally moved when someone reaches out to them with unconditional love that demands nothing in return.

The main thing to remember about servant evangelism is that the initial purpose centers on service. The service rendered is meant to establish an audience with the unchurched. Hopefully, this initial encounter will open a further door of evangelization as the unchurched audience begins to feel less threatened by the development of a hospitable relationship. It is also important to remember that while the initial purpose of this type of evangelism is "service" through acts of hospitality, we are more than "social workers." In the truest sense we are ambassadors for Christ. Therefore our Christian witness should not be a hidden or secondary agenda. To pretend otherwise would not only be hypocritical but a betrayal of our corporate calling and commission as a church. The point is not *whether* to witness for Christ but *when* and *how* to witness.

Intentional acts of hospitality come in all shapes and sizes. While the REACH Team ministry encourages teams to plan specific acts of hospitality, these planned events should never limit any Christian to serve spontaneously when the opportunity arises. For instance, one of our REACH Team participants was doing some shopping on a Saturday morning. The weather was cold and rainy. As this team member began to check out, she noticed a number of people rushing quickly in and out of the grocery store. She had an idea and a big umbrella: "Why not take a few minutes and help these people?" She was a little nervous at first; "What are these people going to think when I offer to share my umbrella in order to keep them dry?"

The first person she approached was an elderly woman. The team member noticed the woman bundling up as she prepared to go out to the parking lot. The team member said, "Excuse me, ma'am, but I noticed that you don't have an umbrella with you this morning." "No, silly me forgot to bring one," she replied. "Can I walk out with you and keep you dry?" The elderly woman was flabbergasted. "Why, young lady, this is one of the nicest things anyone has ever done for me. Why certainly, I will let you walk me out."

The team member discovered that the elderly woman lived in a retirement community just a few miles from our church.

She lived alone and had no immediate relatives in the area. The humble act of kindness deeply moved the heart of the elderly woman. She asked, "Why are you doing this?" The team member replied, "God just put you on my heart this morning when I saw you in the grocery. I knew that I was supposed to help you." Astonishingly the elderly woman became teary-eyed and said, "Young lady, I asked God to give me someone to talk to today, and I believe that he sent you. Thank you for helping me." This team member couldn't believe how God could work so effectively when she made herself available.

The central idea is to perform a specific task in the local community. For instance, a team could provide a "free" gift-wrapping service in a local mall during the Christmas holiday season. As your team wraps gifts, offer shoppers a brochure concerning the ministries of your church. Advertise and promote your church's Christmas programs, pageants, and festival events. While people are waiting, offer them hot chocolate, coffee, or soft drinks. Attempt to strike up casual conversations. And by all means, if someone offers to pay, lovingly and graciously refuse by saying, "This is our way of saying God loves you and so do we! Have a glorious Christmas."

Think about some potential relationships you have, or could easily develop, that could provide evangelistic encounters. If no one comes to mind immediately, don't give up. Ask God to put someone on your heart or in your path with whom you can begin to cultivate an evangelistic relationship.

11

The Priority Involved

Sharing Jesus in a Simple Manner

When it comes to sharing Jesus effectively, many Christians tell themselves, "I cannot do this," or "I'm petrified at the thought of telling someone else about Jesus." Most believers will admit that sharing their personal faith with the unchurched is perhaps the most daunting task of the Christian faith. REACH Team makes the process of sharing one's faith as simple and easy as possible.

REACH Team Uses a Simple, Personal Method to Share the Gospel

REACH Team provides some simple yet effective outlines that present the gospel message clearly without lengthy memorization or "canned" approaches. This helps take the pressure off the witness. A witness is someone who tells the story as it relates specifically to them. Television detective Joe Friday, of the popular TV series *Dragnet*, always spoke this familiar phrase: "Just the facts." That's what the unchurched want to hear—just the facts. And they want to hear them in a simple, authentic manner. That's precisely what a true witness does. He gives an eyewitness account, telling exactly what he has seen or experienced. Believe it or not, our witness does not have to be pages of memorized notes, antidotes, and illustrations that often bear little connection to our lives. Remember: "Just the facts."

REACH Team Requires No Lengthy Memorization Process

Years ago at the first night of a sixteen-week evangelism training course, one of the attendees said, "Preacher, you do know the 'kiss' rule of teaching don't you?" "To be honest, no I don't. What exactly is the 'kiss' rule?" The attendee answered, "Keep it simple, silly!" That attendee held up the seminar notebook and said with a note of concern, "Surely you're not expecting me to memorize all of this?" The person dropped out of the training seminar before it was complete. Why? At first I tried to convince myself that the person wasn't smart enough. Then I told myself that he wasn't committed. Then I reasoned that the person wasn't spiritually minded. Finally, in a state of penned-up frustration, I decided that he probably wasn't even a real Christian!

I went to him and asked, "Why did you drop out?" He said, "Preacher, I truly want to learn how to witness to others with all of my heart. But there are two problems. First, I absolutely cannot memorize that entire notebook. I'm sorry, but I just can't do it. Second, my work and travel schedule will not allow me to commit to the required sixteen weeks of this class." I sensed the frustration and sincere remorse in his words. In a kind yet profound way, he was trying to tell me, "Keep it simple, silly."

Basic Gospel Presentations

REACH Team keeps the presentation of the gospel concise and simple, thereby alleviating the fear of lengthy required memorization work or weeks of scheduled classes. This is in no way an indictment against evangelism training programs that require extensive memorization work and long-term class schedules. I have both attended and facilitated some of these programs. They are effective, thorough, and proficient. From my long-term pastoral experience, however, they do have the propensity to scare away potential participants due to the two primary reasons I've just listed.

Let's take a look at four simple yet precise tools you can utilize in sharing your faith in Jesus Christ. Understand, these are not the only tools available to you. Perhaps you or your church is utilizing an evangelism tool that is not represented in the following pages. That is fine. Use whatever program or method you are familiar with and feel comfortable presenting. These following tools, however, were chosen based upon simplicity, ease of memorization, and clarity of gospel presentation.

A Simple Outline of Your Personal Testimony

Remember that a witness is someone who testifies according to the facts of what he has seen and heard. No greater tool exists for sharing the gospel with the unchurched than your personal story or testimony. It's genuine, personal, and relational. As you develop an authentic relationship with someone who is unchurched, eventually, as social and emotional barriers are removed, that person will allow you to share your salvation experience. The key here is to take time to build trust with the unchurched person. Let them know you personally—your ups and downs, your victories and failures. You do not have to be long-winded to get your point across. (As a rule of thumb, it is best to keep your personal testimony to no more than five minutes.) However, every personal testimony must convey these three imperatives.

- Separation from Christ
- Salvation through Christ
- Security in Christ

First, you must convey the fact that you were at one time separated from God's love. Throughout the Bible we find that humans are by nature sinners separated from a holy God. Paul says, "For all have sinned and fall short of the glory of God" (Rom. 3:23). Share what your life was like without Jesus Christ. Share how sin and unrighteous behavior were predominate in your life prior to your salvation. Finally, share the ultimate result of your life before coming to know Jesus Christ: "For the wages of sin is death" (Rom. 6:23).

Second, convey the fact that you are now a recipient of God's gift of salvation: "But the gift of God is eternal life in Jesus Christ our Lord" (Rom. 6:23). Share the fact that Jesus Christ died for your sins on the cross. Share that "God demonstrated his own love for us in this: While we were still sinners, Christ died for us" (Rom. 5:8). Let your listener know that you are now forgiven and cleansed of all your sins, not because of anything you have done, but because of what God did for you through his Son.

Third, share how your life has been changed dramatically since you have become a believer and follower of Jesus Christ. Let the listener know that God's salvation is forever: "Therefore, he is able to save completely those who have come to God through him, because he always lives to intercede for them" (Heb. 7:25). Share the promise of Scripture that God will never let you down, never leave you alone, and never give up on you: "Never will I leave you; never will I forsake you" (Heb. 13:5). Most important is the fact that your personal testimony cannot be disputed. It is the authentic reality of

God's supernatural transformation of your life. You're not simply telling someone about what happened to someone else but to you personally. Take a few minutes to ponder your personal salvation experience. Afterward, write out your testimony using the simple guideline provided below.

Separation from Christ

_____

_____

_____

_____

_____

_____

_____

_____

Salvation through Christ

_____

_____

_____

_____

_____

_____

Security in Christ

_____

_____

_____

_____

_____

_____

Memorize the Presentation of "One Verse Evangelism"

One of the easiest and most effective witnessing tools available to believers today is the "One Verse Evangelism" presentation.[1] This simple gospel presentation uses one verse of Scripture, Romans 6:23, presented in an illustrative diagram, to explain the message of salvation:

> For the wages of sin is death,
> but the gift of God is eternal life
> in Christ Jesus our Lord.

Let's break this verse down by detailing the key words in this verse in order to understand completely its message.

Wages

We receive wages for what we have done. It is something we earn for a job or deed we perform.

Sin

Sin means "to miss the mark." Simply stated, sin is when we fall short of living a good or perfect life before God.

Death

Death refers to a final and irreversible separation from God as a result of the wages of our sinful behavior on earth.

But

This is the most important word in this verse because it indicates there is hope for all of us. What we have presented so far is bad news, but God has good news.

Gift

A gift is something that someone gives to you freely; it costs you nothing. In this case, the gift is salvation through God's Son, Jesus Christ.

Of God

This free gift comes directly from God himself, the Creator and sustainer of the universe. Remember: Only God can give this type of gift.

Eternal Life

This means two things. First, it means *quantity* of life. When you receive God's free gift of salvation through Jesus Christ, you will live forever in a place called heaven. It also means *quality* of life. Jesus offers a life like no other. Just as separation from God starts in this life and extends into eternity, eternal life starts now and goes on forever. No sin can end it.

Jesus Christ

Jesus is the only means by which we can receive eternal life. No one can offer a gift except the one who purchases it, and Jesus purchased it with his life on the cross called Calvary. Close out your presentation with one additional word that is not used within the actual verse . . .

ONE VERSE EVANGELISM

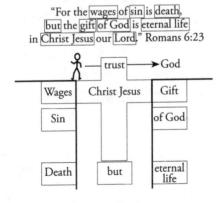

"For the wages of sin is death, but the gift of God is eternal life in Christ Jesus our Lord." Romans 6:23

153

Trust

We have not lived life the way God would want us to. We deserve death as a payment for our sins; however, if we trust (*believe*) that Jesus took our punishment for us, we are forgiven. On the previous page is a visible illustration that you can use to explain this one verse. This illustration can be drawn on a scratch piece of paper, a napkin, or copied and used as a small evangelism tract.

Memorize the Presentation of "The Handout"

Presenting the gospel can be as easy as using your hand, literally! In this case, you use your hand to illustrate the message of salvation through Jesus Christ much like a person

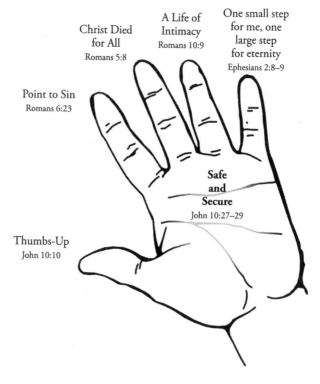

154

who offers a "free handout," or gift. Each of your five fingers and the palm of your hand represent a specific truth related to salvation in Christ.[2]

Your Thumb

Represents "thumbs-up." Most people remember the popular sitcom from the early seventies, *Happy Days*. One of the main characters of the show was Fonzie, a rebel of sorts, who often signaled his approval and acceptance of something by a thumbs-up. Here, the thumbs-up is a sign of approval, or in this case, Good News! The gospel is Good News. Jesus said in John 10:10, "I have come that they may have life, and have it to the full." The message of salvation is a free gift given only by Jesus that signifies a full and meaningful life.

Your Pointer Finger

The pointer finger is sometimes used to indicate the beginning point of something. In this case, the beginning point of salvation begins when we recognize that we are all sinners and cannot save ourselves. "For the wages of sin is death, but the gift of God is eternal life in Christ Jesus our Lord" (Rom. 6:23).

Your Middle Finger

The middle finger is longer than all the others. In this case, Christ's love and sacrifice on the cross overshadows, or covers, all our sins. "But God demonstrated his love for us in this: While we were still sinners, Christ died for us" (Rom. 5:8).

Your Ring Finger

The ring finger has traditionally been used as the one where we place the symbol of our commitment to another person—a wedding ring. In this case, this is a symbol of our personal intimacy with Jesus Christ as our Savior and Lord, namely, that we enter into an intimate relationship with him. "That if you confess with your mouth, 'Jesus is Lord,' and believe in your heart that God raised him from the dead, you will be saved" (Rom. 10:9).

Your Pinky Finger

Your smallest finger represents the relatively small step of faith that we must take in order to accept the great gift that God offers us; eternal life with him. Remember: Eternal life doesn't begin when you die; it begins when you accept him. "For it is by grace you have been saved, through faith—and this not from yourselves, it is the gift of God—not by works, so that no one can boast" (Eph. 2:8–9).

Your Palm

The palm of your hand represents the safety and security that only God can provide. This is the eternal promise of salvation through Jesus Christ. For Christ himself said, "My sheep listen to my voice; I know them, and they follow me. I give them eternal life, and they shall never perish; no one can snatch them out of my hand. My Father, who has given them to me, is greater than all; no one can snatch them out of my Father's hand" (John 10:27–29).

You close your presentation by asking, "Would you like to receive the free handout of salvation through Jesus Christ right now?" Often, it is good to extend your hand (palm up) to the person you are witnessing to in order to demonstrate the simplicity of receiving God's free gift of forgiveness and salvation.

Your Life: A New Beginning
(North American Mission Board of the Southern Baptist Convention)

The North American Mission Board of the Southern Baptist Convention has designed an effective gospel presentation entitled *Your Life: A New Beginning.*[3] The following is an abbreviated outline of the full gospel tract.

1. God is interested in your life story.

- He created you (Ps. 139:13–14).
- He knows you (Ps. 139:1–3).
- He loves you (John 3:16).
- He has a plan for you (John 10:10).

God wants to fill your life story with meaning now and to give you his gift of eternal life.

Why then are most people not experiencing the full and meaningful life that God offers?

2. Our sins separate us from God.

- All of us are sinners (Rom. 3:23).
- Our punishment for sin is death (Rom. 6:23).

No person is truly "good" based on God's standard—which is perfection.

What then is the secret to receiving God's gift of eternal life?

3. The secret is found in Jesus. He can change your life story.

- Jesus is God (John 1:1–2, 14).
- Jesus died on the cross for you (1 Cor. 15:3–4).
- Jesus in the only way to God (John 14:6).

Jesus wants to be the author of your life. How does that happen?

4. Receive Jesus Christ as your Savior and Lord.

- Personally receive Jesus (John 1:12).
- Repent of your sins (Acts 3:19).
- Place your faith in Jesus (Eph. 2:8–9).

Would you like to make Jesus the author of your life today?

There is another tool I wish to recommend that is simple, brief, and powerful in its presentation. Frank Harbor and Ken Hemphill developed an evangelism presentation called www.gotlife.org. This online tool is a dynamic presentation geared toward our postmodern seeker. The tool provides an interactive guide that leads the seeker through the complete gospel presentation and then records the decision for future follow-up. I highly recommend you visit this website and check it out as a potential tool you can implement in your witnessing strategy.

In closing this chapter, let's focus on actually leading a person to personal profession of faith in Jesus Christ. By this point in your witnessing effort, you have helped the unsaved person understand the basic elements of saving faith. Now comes the crucial point of the witnessing encounter—inviting the unsaved person to make a faith-based commitment of his or her life to the Lord Jesus Christ. There are three basic steps that you should include in this act:

Understanding
Praying
Reassuring

First, make sure that the unsaved person understands the basis of salvation. The key is *not* to rush the encounter. Make sure that the unsaved person understands and is receptive. Never force the gospel on someone. Remember, the central ingredient of the gospel encounter is in the role of the Holy Spirit to convict and convince. We cannot manipulate or coerce a person to salvation. If we do, we run the risk of misleading a person to a false or insincere profession.

Don't hesitate to review the basics of the plan of salvation at this point. Also, don't be afraid to allow the unsaved person to ask questions. I know what some of you are thinking at this point: "I'm afraid he or she will ask me a question that I cannot answer!" That's okay. Don't let a potentially unanswerable question keep you from leading an unsaved person to Christ. If you don't know the answer to the question, just say, "I'm sorry, but I don't know the answer to that question." At this point, just go right back to your gospel presentation. Stay on track with what you *do* know. You can always offer to find out the answer to the question and get back in touch at a later date.

The next step is to lead the unsaved person in a prayer of faith. While there is no specific pattern to this prayer, some key elements need to be included in the prayer:

- Admit you are a sinner.
- Believe that Jesus is God's Son and did rise from the dead.
- Confess your faith and trust in Jesus Christ to forgive and cleanse you.

Most of the time it is good to lead the unsaved person in this prayer. The easiest way is for you to pray the prayer and have the unsaved person repeat the prayer. A short, very basic confession (prayer) of faith could be the following example:

Dear Lord Jesus,
I confess that I am a sinner.
I believe that you are God's Son who died and rose again.
Please forgive me of all my sins, and come into my life and
save me.
Thank you, Lord, for saving my soul. Amen.

The final step is to reassure the new Christian of his or
her salvation in Christ. Remind the person that God's love
and forgiveness is unconditional and eternal. Affirm to the
person that God holds them in his hand (John 10:27–29),
and promises to never leave or forsake them (Heb. 13:5).

Now comes the ever-important step of follow-up. Too
many times have we seen and heard about individuals making professions of faith but never being followed up properly.
The friendship you have cultivated will aid in the future dis-
cipleship and nurturing of the new believer. It is extremely
important to stay in continual contact with the new believer.
Invite the person to your Bible study or Sunday school class.
Encourage the person to attend worship regularly. If your
church offers a new believers' class, then enroll the person in
the class. Just as a newborn baby needs constant attention,
so does a new Christian. You must maintain a positive and
consistent relationship with the new believer.

Remember this: The most important thing about sharing
your faith is not the *method* you use but the *motivation* of
your heart! In other words, it's not a question of *how* you
share but *why* you share.

12

The Power Involved

Learning to Pray for the Unchurched

Perhaps the greatest empowering element within the church apart from the Holy Spirit is the ministry of prayer. In fact, prayer is an indispensable ingredient for any church that desires to be a kingdom-minded force for the glory of Jesus Christ. Unfortunately, prayer is often the most omitted ministry in the local church. Estimates state that the average Christian prays less than two minutes a day. Even worse, the average pastor prays less than five minutes a day. And when Christians do pray, it is often vague and superficial: "Lord, bless our church," or "Lord, save the world." Real prayer is vastly different from "cliche praying" that does little more than ask God to bless your cornflakes or heal your ingrown toenail.

I'm absolutely convinced that one primary reason the church is not reaching the masses as it should is that it has lost the practice of praying for the unchurched. Sure, we offer lip service in our prayers for the lost; especially when we have a special focus on missions or evangelism in our churches. But how many of us really pray specifically for lost people by name? How many of us truly plead with the Lord for the lost souls of unsaved people all around us? And how many of us pray that the Lord will give us soul-winning encounters in our daily lives? Praying for the lost and unchurched should be a daily part of our lives. When someone you know and love doesn't know Christ, it should be natural to pray for his or her salvation.

In Matthew 9:38, the Lord Jesus tells his disciples to "ask the Lord of the harvest, therefore, to send out workers into his harvest field." Here we see the Lord's command for us to pray for workers as they depart into the harvest fields. Some have said that while the Lord instructs us to pray for harvesters, nowhere in Scripture are we instructed to pray specifically for "unsaved people." There are two primary problems with this mind-set. First, we are given both the example and instruction to pray regarding the harvest. Second, once we justify not praying for the unchurched, it becomes quite easy to neglect that important dimension of our Christian lives, because fervent evangelistic prayer takes time and energy and will lead to involvement.

The Bible is full of examples where individuals prayed fervently for the salvation and redemption of wayward souls. For instance, in the Old Testament, Moses prayed in Numbers 11:1–2 for God not to consume the unbelieving, complaining Israelites in fiery judgment. In Numbers 14:19, Moses cries out to God, saying, "In accordance with your great love, forgive the sin of these people, just as you have pardoned them from the time they have left Egypt until now." Moses, a man of God and the appointed leader of Israel, expressed to God his heart's burning desire for Israel's salvation and deliverance.

In 1 Samuel 12:23–25, Samuel says to the Israelites, "As for me, far be it from me that I should sin against the LORD by failing to pray for you. And I will teach you the way that is good and right. But be sure to fear the LORD and serve him faithfully with all your heart; consider what great things he has done for you. Yet if you persist in doing what is evil, both you and your king will be swept away." Samuel was saying not only that his praying for the Israelites was important but that it was sin *not* to pray. From the testimony of Jeremiah, we know that a major part of his prophetic ministry was crying to God on behalf of his people. Unfortunately, the Israelites had continued in their sin so long that God told Jeremiah to stop praying for them (Jer. 7:13–16).

In the New Testament we find Stephen stoned to death for what the Jewish people saw as blasphemy—the gospel of Jesus Christ. As he was being stoned to death, he asked the Lord to receive him, and then he prayed this incredible prayer: "Lord, do not hold this sin against them" (Acts 7:60), which is to say, "God, please be merciful on these sinners." In Romans 9:2 the apostle Paul said that he had "great sorrow and unceasing anguish in his heart." He goes on in verses 3–4 to exhort, "For I wish that I myself were cursed and cut off from Christ for the sake of my brothers, those of my own race, the people of Israel." Later in Romans 10:1 Paul laments, "Brothers, my heart's desire and prayer to God for the Israelites is that they may be saved."

Praying for the Unsaved

One of the clearest passages of Scripture concerning praying for the lost is found in 1 Timothy 2:1–8. These eight verses contain three primary propositions: (1) Christians should pray for the salvation of all people (v. 1), (2) God wants all people to be saved (v. 4), and (3) believers must meet certain conditions to pray acceptably (v. 8). The main point of the passage is that the church is called to pray for the lost on a wide scale. First Timothy 2:1 gives us the basis of our prayer for the unsaved, described in four key words from that verse that offer direct reference to our praying for the lost:

Requests

The word *request* infers a lack of something, or a great need of something. When a person lacks something that he needs, he goes to the place where he can fill that need. In this case, evangelistic praying rises from a deep sense of need for salvation for the lost. As Christians, we know that the lost are without God's love and ultimately doomed for eternal damnation. Our *requests* are a heartfelt response to the need of salvation for all people. The lost have a great need for forgiveness and salvation, and our *requests* before the Father are meant to meet that need.

Prayers

Prayer is a specific word for praying that is addressed solely to the Father. The idea conveyed is that of worship and respect. In this case, we pray for lost souls not only because of their tremendous need but because of God's matchless glory and honor. It is God who receives the glory when a lost person comes to faith in Christ. We pray but God gets the glory. When we pray for the salvation of others, we seek God to get the glory and praise that is due only unto him.

Intercessions

The word *intercession* expresses the idea of someone praying on behalf of another person. This denotes a degree of personal intimacy toward another. Simply stated, we should pray for the salvation of others with deep compassion, not routine rhetoric. In the average church, when we pray for the salvation of others, it is usually performed by a blanket request such as, "Lord, save all the people in our city," or

"Lord, please save all the lost souls around the world." Very rarely do we ever pray specifically for a lost person by name. Something about praying specifically for a person's salvation makes it more personal and demonstrates an authentic compassion on our part.

In November 2002 I attended a prayer summit. One of the keynote speakers for the event was Kathleen Grant.[1] She is truly an amazing woman when it comes to the ministry of prayer. During that prayer summit, Kathleen stated that she prays for about twenty-five hundred lost people by name every week! When I heard her say that, my initial reaction was "No way; that's impossible." But the more I was exposed to her teaching and ministry, the more I realized Kathleen clearly understood the call to pray for the unchurched.

Her testimony had two dramatic effects upon me. First, it utterly shamed me. I was truly convicted by the Holy Spirit. I had to confess before God that I wasn't praying for any lost people specifically by name. Yes, I was praying to God for souls to be saved, but suddenly I realized how incredibly vague my prayers were. Second, I was motivated to begin praying for lost people specifically by name. I went back to my office the next day and began a list of people I knew were unsaved and began praying for them. I now maintain a list of unsaved people whom I pray for specifically.

Thanksgiving

The word *thanksgiving* denotes the idea of giving or showing thanks to God for the privilege we have of reaching others with the gospel message of Jesus Christ. That's right; it is our privilege to share the Good News with unsaved people. God has so ordained each of us within the body of Christ to show and share our faith with the unchurched. And we ought to thank God daily for such an opportunity, to both pray for and share the gospel message with the lost.

How to Pray Specifically

Let's take a moment and outline some steps concerning our praying for the lost and unchurched. While these steps are in no specific order, they all play a significant part in your daily praying for lost souls.

1. Make a list of people you know who are unsaved and begin praying for them by name. Can you imagine what would happen in the average church if each member of that congregation began praying specifically for lost people? Who are some people in your circle of influence who are unsaved and in need of prayer? Start a prayer journal for the unsaved people in your life.

2. Pray that God will give you people to pray for. Many times I hear Christians say, "I don't know any lost people to pray for." My response to them is, "Why not?" We come into contact with hundreds of people every week. Many, if not most, of those people are unsaved. Get to know them by name. Ask God to begin revealing people to you who are unsaved.

3. Pray that God will give you opportunities to share your faith. Ask God for the privilege to share your faith in him with someone. Ask God to bring a lost soul into your life. I am convinced that each day holds "divine appointments" for all of us. Unfortunately, because we are not praying for them or looking for them, they often pass us by. When you are praying for opportunities to share your faith, you will be forced to be on the alert by constantly asking, "Lord, is this the one you have sent to me today?"

4. Stay "confessed up" and clean from sin. While God is more than apt and ready to use a vessel that is broken, he will not use a dirty vessel. Sadly many of us miss out on witnessing opportunities due to the unconfessed sin in our lives. In essence, we void ourselves out completely from God's purpose and evangelistic plan for us. What unconfessed sin is there in your heart right now that is keeping you from being effective in God's evangelistic plan for your life?

5. Pray that God will give you supernatural boldness to share when the opportunity arises. Over the years, one of the greatest excuses I have heard from would-be witnesses is "I'm just not bold enough to share my faith." What they fail to understand is that they actually stand in pretty good company when they confess their lack of boldness. Remember in Acts 4 when the apostles were put in jail for preaching the gospel? The rulers of the synagogue threatened their lives if they continued to preach. This would have probably caused any rationally minded person to stop preaching. I'm sure that in the minds of these apostles they began to question their reason for proclaiming the gospel. However, instead of cowering in fear, they prayed for more boldness to share their faith (Acts 4:29–31). When we are faced with daunting, disturbing circumstances that potentially serve to derail our faith, we also need to pray for spiritual boldness.

6. Pray that Christ will be reflected through your life each day. A vital part of our bold witness is the ability to reflect Christ through our actions. Simply stated, "Let others see Jesus in you." The old cliche is quite true: "Actions speak louder than words."

7. Pray that God will fill you daily with his love and grace. It is virtually impossible to share your faith when your love for others has grown cold. For this reason alone we need to ask God daily to fill our hearts with his love and grace. Have you noticed that it's easier to share your faith with someone you love and respect? But what about the person at work who is obnoxious, crude, or disrespectful? That person needs Jesus too. What about the family member who is always complaining, griping, or belittling others? That person needs Jesus. What about the neighbor who never smiles, never waves hello, or never engages in conversation? Are you getting the picture? Understand that God never commissions us to share our faith only with the people we like. We must be willing to love the unlovely, embrace the unkind, and accept those who are different from us.

The biblical picture of this type of evangelistic encounter is found in Saul's conversion experience. Acts 9:1–19 reveals the story of Saul's dramatic conversion experience while on the road to Damascus. Saul, the great persecutor of the saints, was well known throughout the land for his hatred against the church of Jesus Christ. Yet God, in his infinite mercy and grace, saw fit to call out Saul on the Damascus road. The Lord told Saul to go to Damascus and wait for his instruction. At the same time, the Lord spoke to a believer named Ananias and told him to meet Saul in Damascus and lay his hands upon him in order to restore Saul's sight. The response that Ananias gave the Lord is interesting. "'Lord,' Ananias answered, 'I have heard many reports about this man and all the harm he has done to your saints in Jerusalem. And he has come here with authority from the chief priests to arrest all who call on your name'" (Acts 9:13–14).

In effect, Ananias was saying, "Lord, are you sure you've got the right guy? I mean, after all, Saul is a persecutor of the saints and a real thorn in the side of the church." While one could say that Ananias's attitude was self-righteous and judgmental, the evidence was overwhelmingly in favor of his evaluation of Saul. Saul was anything but the perfect picture of someone likely to know and follow Jesus. In fact, he was the complete opposite. No wonder Ananias was leery about Saul's conversion.

8. *Pray for more laborers to go into the harvest fields.* Jesus instructed the early believers to pray diligently for laborers to go into the harvest fields (Matt. 9:37–38). The sad reality is that we live in a lost, hell-bound world full of hurting people. Jesus said that the masses of lost people were enormous. He also presented a problem; the laborers were very few. Jesus never told us to panic or even invent a great church program. He simply tells us to "Ask [pray] the Lord of the harvest, therefore, to send out workers into his harvest fields" (Matt. 9:38, brackets mine). It's amazing that we are to ask the "Lord of the harvest"—the great Judge—to send workers into the

harvest fields in order to keep people from the impending judgment to come. While God's holiness demands justice, his love desires that no one receive it.

Interestingly, Jesus didn't command the disciples to pray for the "lost," although that is certainly appropriate. He told them to pray for *laborers*. Think about God's method for a moment. First, God wants us to understand that people are lost and few are available to reach them. Second, he wants us to pray for him to send people to reach the lost with the gospel. If you pray for laborers long enough, eventually God will enlist you. And remember, one person can have an amazing impact on the harvest when he gets involved in the Lord's work. We are to intercede on behalf of the lost by asking God to send laborers and then to say like Isaiah, "Here am I. Send me" (Isa. 6:8).

13

The Passion Involved

The Responsibility of Being Accountable before God and Others

Many of those who monitor our social patterns say that we are living in a passionless age. Our pluralistic culture embraces everything yet commits to nothing. Most people are comfortable with their commonplace, routine lifestyles. They are satisfied with passionless lives, emotionless relationships, and fruitless endeavors. However, we are not completely void of passion. Inevitably, every week, tens of thousands of fans will pack stadiums watching their favorite teams battle it out.

Being from Kentucky, I grew up with a great passion for basketball. One of my all-time favorite players is Michael Jordan. Until Jordan arrived on the NBA scene, the standard contract for an NBA player included a clause that prevented any off-season basketball participation without approval from team management. Jordan's contract had to be written differently because he refused to concede that part of his life. He became the first player to have what is called the "love of the game" clause. It permitted him complete freedom to play basketball year-round, more precisely, during the off-season.

Of course, such a request was befitting a man who practiced as hard as he played. By his own admission, Jordan once stated, "I never stopped trying to get better."[1] It's little wonder such a raw passion for the game of basketball led Jordan to score over twenty-nine thousand points and win five MVP awards and six NBA championships. It also explains his unforgettable performance in the 1997 play-off game with the Utah Jazz. He was ravaged by the flu but still scored an amazing thirty-eight points and made the game-winning three-pointer even though pain, fever, and severe dehydration caused him to collapse several times when leaving the game.[2]

The dictionary offers various definitions of *passion*, including, "any powerful emotion or appetite," "an abandoned display of emotion," and "boundless enthusiasm."[3] I believe that the biblical definition for the word *passion* takes the idea to a greater level of understanding. The Greek word for passion, *pascho*, in the New Testament is used predominately in reference to one who willfully suffers on behalf of another.[4] In the Christian community we are all familiar with Passion Week, the time period between Christ's arrival in Jerusalem and his impending crucifixion. It is known as Passion Week because of the excruciating pain, torture, and ultimate death that Jesus experienced for all humankind. In other words, Jesus was passionate, even to the point of death, for the cause for which he was sent. As I reflect upon the passion that Jesus displayed for our salvation, I have to ask the question, "Where is the passion for souls in our churches today?"

Take a look at the following statistics provided by the North American Mission Board of the Southern Baptist Convention. Certainly these figures support the growing need for Christians to become more passionate in their evangelization in North America:

- Estimated U.S. unchurched population: 195,000,000 people.
- Estimated U.S. unsaved population: 160,000,000 people.
- During the 10-year period from the mid 1980s to mid 1990s, the U.S. population has increased 11.4 percent while church membership declined 9.5 percent.
- Church attendance has declined approximately 10 percent over the last ten years.
- No county in North America has a greater percentage of churched people today than a decade ago.
- North America is the only continent where Christianity is not growing.
- There is a net loss of forty-eight churches per week in North America, or nearly seven churches per day.[5]

This sampling of statistics shows the unprecedented need for evangelistic effectiveness. Unfortunately, if we choose to get honest with ourselves, we must admit that we (the church generally and Christians specifically) are not doing a favorable job of transforming our society or local communities. What is the culprit of this lack of effectiveness? I believe it is summed up in one word: *passivity.*

Jesus condemned the unmotivated servant who passively buried his talent in the sand. Evangelistic passivity denies the urgency of humankind's greatest need—salvation through Jesus Christ.

Developing a "Passion" for Souls

It often takes God longer to get a Christian ready and available to witness than it does to get a lost person ready to receive the gospel. The salvation experience of a lost person consists of three vital elements: (1) the Gospel presentation of Jesus Christ, (2) the supernatural work of the Holy Spirit who is able to bring conviction upon the heart of a lost sinner, and (3) the involvement of human evangelization. God has ordained that Christians proclaim the message of salvation to a lost and dying world. The first two elements are always alive and active in the conversion process. However, the third element is seriously lacking today.

The primary place to start is the example of Jesus Christ. Jesus had an overwhelming passion for lost souls. His passion was driven by a "compassion" for those who were lost. Matthew 9:36 records that when Jesus saw the multitudes, "He had compassion on them." The word *compassion* comes from the Latin, *patior*, meaning "to suffer," or "to feel," and the prefix *com* means "with someone else." Therefore, when we have compassion, we suffer or feel for someone else, namely, regarding a person's condition or state of being.[6] This is exactly what Jesus did. He suffered with (and ultimately on behalf of) lost humankind.

Developing a passion for lost souls is conceived through a compassionate spirit from within. Just as Jesus wept over the multitudes (Luke 19:41), we too must hunger for a compassionate spirit to captivate us so that we might also weep for the lost. The psalmist wrote:

> Those who sow in tears
>   will reap with songs of joy.
> He who goes out weeping,
>   carrying seed to sow,
> will return with songs of joy,
>   carrying sheaves with him.
>
> Psalm 126:5–6

How can we develop a burden and compassion for the lost? Take a few moments and read the following suggestions, and allow the simple truth of each statement to saturate your heart, mind, and spirit.

Remember That No One Has the Promise of Tomorrow

The sad but true reality is that none of us have the absolute promise or guarantee of tomorrow. James, the half brother of Jesus, wrote, "Why, you do not even know what will happen tomorrow. What is your life? You are a mist that appears for a little while and then vanishes" (James 4:14).

Realize That People Outside of Christ Are Destined to Eternal Damnation

Hebrews 9:27 says, "Just as a man is destined to die once, and after that to face judgment." I was fascinated to read that according to a recent poll conducted by the Barna Research Group, 76 percent of Americans believe in heaven and 71 percent believe in hell. However, what was even more fascinating was the fact that 64 percent of our American society believes that when they die, they will go to heaven. Interestingly, only one-half of 1 percent said that they were hell-bound, according to the national survey.[7] Think about that: less than one half of 1 percent of our American population thinks they are destined for hell.

This postmodern, humanistic, pluralistic, mind-set contradicts completely what Jesus said about the eternal existence of the vast majority of people who have lived on this earth: "Enter through the narrow gate. For wide is the gate and broad is the road that leads to destruction, and *many* enter through it. But small is the gate and narrow is the road that leads to life, and only a few find it" (Matt. 7:13–14, emphasis mine). Hell is a reality, regardless of what our lost and dying world wants to believe.

A member of the first church I served after completing my seminary degree magnified this picture to me. John was a single man who had lived a horrible life for years before coming to Christ. One day John came by my office and asked me if he could tell me about his conversion experience in Christ. I welcomed John into my office, and he began telling me one of the most amazing stories I had ever heard. A few years earlier, John was living in Phoenix, Arizona. He was not a Christian at the time. In fact, he was a hard-hearted alcoholic who was bitter about life. One day John suffered a massive heart attack and was rushed to the hospital. The hospital attendants quickly rushed John to the emergency room and began administering care. At this point in telling his story, John's eyes began to tear up, and he said:

> Preacher, I died on that hospital table that day. I didn't see any bright lights, angels, or saints calling me to heaven. What I saw scared me beyond death. It was very dark, with just a deep orange glow from the fire in the background. It was so hot that I could hardly breathe. My skin felt like it was on fire. All I could hear was people screaming and yelling, "Save me, save me. Please, someone save me!" All around me there were eerie, indescribable creatures that were tormenting me. I could not get away from them. I was so thirsty that my tongue stuck to the roof of my mouth. My body ached all over as if somebody was hitting me with clubs. And I began to scream out, "Save me, save me. Someone please save me!"

John then told me that the emergency room doctors resuscitated him miraculously. A few days later, John woke up in a hospital room and immediately cried out for a hospital chaplain to come to his room. The hospital chaplain did come, and John said, "I've been to hell, and I don't ever want to go back. Please, help me find Jesus!" That day the hospital chaplain led John to pray and receive Jesus Christ as his Savior and Lord.

That's an astonishing story to say the least, I thought to myself, but John wasn't finished. He told me that after he had completely recovered from his heart attack, he moved back to Brunswick, Georgia, to live with his ailing mother. John's mother, Edith, was also a member of my first church. When John arrived at his mother's home, he shared his life-changing experience with her. John told me that Edith began to cry with great joy. She told him, "John, God has answered my prayers for you. I've been praying for over thirty years for God to save you. I became so desperate, I asked God to show you what was awaiting you in eternity if you didn't accept Jesus." John said that when his mother told him about her prayer request, he began to weep uncontrollably. He said that they both sat there weeping together, but that they were not tears of sorrow. Rather, they were tears of great joy. John said to me, "Preacher, God loved me enough that he was willing to show me what hell was going to be like in order to get me to come to Jesus."

If every true believer could spend five minutes in hell, would it change our attitude and passion toward reaching the lost? Perhaps. One thing is for certain—we must be more conscious of the fact that every single day thousands and thousands of souls are being lost to an eternal damnation. The gospel is Good News! People are hungry for the truth. While people are hungry to hear the gospel, they are also unconcerned about the eternal consequences of hell. This perspective should motivate us even more to go forth with the message of salvation and share it with every lost person on the face of the earth.

Redirect Our Worldly View of Society to a Biblical Worldview

What do I mean when I say "biblical worldview"? Simply this: We need to start seeing the world through the eyes of Jesus. We must face the reality that much of our world has become increasingly unchurched due to the ineffectiveness of its churches. George Barna indicates that there is virtually "no difference" in the lives of the people of God and the society around them. It is Barna's opinion that Christians are no longer making a significant difference, morally or even spiritually, in our culture. "Our influence as salt and light is quickly becoming compromised."[8] Barna offers a clear-cut definition of a "biblical worldview":

A *biblical worldview* is a means of experiencing, interpreting, and responding to reality in light of biblical perspective. This life lens provides a personal understanding of every idea, opportunity, and experience based on the identification and application of relevant biblical principles so that every choice we make may be consistent with God's principles and commands. At the risk of seeming simplistic, it is asking the question, "What would Jesus do if He were in my shoes right now?" and applying the answer without compromising because of how we anticipate the world reacting.[9]

While this definition entails the total picture of what the Christian community should strive for, my thought primarily focuses on how we look specifically at the lost community around us. In other words, the Christian community must see our lost society as Jesus saw them. We often see our lost society as rebellious and overindulgent. Moreover, many within the Christian community see our world as virtually nothing more than a lost cause with just a remnant of people who have a true shot at real salvation.

The Scriptures say, "When he [Jesus] saw the crowds, he had compassion on them, because they were harassed and helpless, like sheep without a shepherd" (Matt. 9:36). Perhaps we should start seeing the unchurched community not as hindrances to the moral, ethical, and spiritual standard we seek for our society, or as mere numbers that serve to increase our church membership rolls. We should see them with the compassion and sensitivity that Jesus saw them, as those who are "harassed and helpless, like sheep without a shepherd." We've got to love the lost to faith in Jesus Christ. We've got to reach out to them, befriending, embracing, and accepting them as they are. I'm not suggesting we condone sinful behaviors or ungodly lifestyles of unbelievers. But we cannot afford to condemn the lost to hell by simply giving up on them because of their sin and indifference.

Replenish the Time You Spend with the Unchurched

Too many Christians have no close relationships with the unchurched. A common response that Christians offer when asked if they have any unsaved friends is, "Why do I want to associate with lost people? They're a bad influence on me. They'll only bring me down in my faith." Interestingly some of the best prospects come through the "recently saved" new members of the church. Why? Because prior to their salvation experience in Christ, virtually all of their friends were lost people.

When one becomes a Christian, why do we often think we're no longer permitted to associate with the unsaved? It is true that when a person comes to Christ there should be a supernatural change in one's life. Paul wrote to the Corinthian church, "Therefore, if anyone is in Christ, he is a new creation; the old has gone, the new has come!" (2 Cor. 5:17). Our lives as Christians should strive for righteousness, holiness, and purity. But does that mean we exclude everybody from our lives who has yet to be saved?

Jesus said, "You are the light of the world. A city on a hill cannot be hidden. Neither do people light a lamp and put it under a bowl. Instead they put it on its stand, and it gives light to everyone in the house. In the same way, let your light shine before men, that they may see your good deeds and praise your Father in heaven" (Matt. 5:14–16). God's people are to proclaim and display God's light in a world engulfed in darkness. A hidden Christian is as incongruous as a hidden light.

Ask God to Give You a Burden for the Lost

Can you imagine what would happen in America if every evangelical pastor would truly begin to seek God for a genuine burden for lost people? Can you imagine what could happen in your church if just a handful of people got serious about reaching lost people and began begging God for a heavy burden for the lost people in their local community? I firmly believe that we would see the beginnings of a nationwide revival—a supernatural, unexplainable movement of God.

Every revival in the history of the world has been grounded in an explosion of brokenness in prayer and a burden for lost souls.

Why don't you put this book down for a minute and ask God to give you a burden for someone who is lost? Stop right now and ask God to give you that person's name, and begin praying for his or her soul to be saved. Pray for that person again tomorrow, and the next day, and the next. . . . Keep praying for that person until God gives you a deep burden for that person's soul. Then you will begin to see people come to Christ. Then you will begin to see a harvest of souls. Then you will see and experience the mighty moving of the Holy Spirit in your community.

Passion Builds the Stepping-Stones of Team Accountability

History shows us that Christian evangelism is not always enthusiastically received. All but one of the Lord's apostles were martyred. Since that time it is estimated that over forty million Christians have been martyred because they promoted and defended their faith.[10] Why? The answer lies in the depth of their understanding of and accountability toward the Christian faith.

In our postmodern world, success has been defined in fleshly, materialistic, and earthly ways—popularity, wealth, power, fame, comfort, individualism, and the attainment of possessions. Increasingly more and more people abide by the notion that it takes a combination of these characteristics or achievements to garner real success.

Heaven regards success in a different manner altogether. Jesus defined success two thousand years ago during his earthly ministry; and before that, God defined success when he revealed his will for the Israelites. Biblical success can be defined as *faithfulness (accountability) and obedience to God*. Everything else is secondary at best. In the end, all that will matter is whether we yielded our lives completely to God and gave him our faithful service as good stewards.

Jesus challenged his disciples to "count the cost" (see Luke 14:25–33) before following him. Paul would later challenge those in the Corinthian church to "examine yourselves" (2 Cor. 13:5; namely, "give an account") to see if their actions and deeds matched their faith and knowledge of true salvation. In both accounts, we find a sense of personal and corporate accountability to Christ and also the church.

Who are you accountable to when it comes to your faithful, obedient, and responsible service? Obviously we know and adhere to the fact that we, as followers of Christ, are accountable to him as our righteous judge. In fact, we will give an account of our lives before him at the judgment seat (1 Cor. 3:10–15). But who holds you accountable right now? Does someone in your life now help motivate, challenge, and stir you in your evangelistic efforts?

The team approach to REACH provides a built-in accountability system unlike other types of evangelism ministries. Each person has a personal support base to build upon. Team members become accountable and responsible to one another as they seek to reach out to their lost and unchurched family members, friends, and neighbors. Team members build on one another's strengths and offset one another's weaknesses.

If you want to see an excellent example of teamwork, observe the giant redwood trees in California. These trees can grow to heights exceeding three hundred feet. You would think that they need a deep root system. Not so. Redwoods have very shallow root systems that capture all of the surface moisture possible. Because these roots spread out in hundreds of directions, the roots of all the trees are intertwined. As a result, one tree supports another tree, and they help each other stand, even in high winds and torrential rains. That is why you rarely see a redwood standing alone. They need one another to thrive and survive.[11]

Teamwork in the church, especially as it relates to evangelistic efforts, helps build support and accountability. Team members feed off of the passion for souls that others share. That passion serves to motivate, challenge, and encourage others to do likewise in their personal witness.

14

The Price Involved

Dealing with Questions and Handling Rejections

At times God permits his children to be witnesses in situations where they run the risk of physical, social, and emotional harm. For instance, look at the early apostles. They were all maligned, ostracized, and ridiculed for their faith. In 2 Corinthians 11:23–29, the apostle Paul details the tragic experiences he endured as a result of proclaiming the gospel. Millions have died through the centuries as a result of commitment to their faith.

Today the vast majority of Christians in the United States do not worry about losing their life as a direct result of their personal testimony. However, there is still a great fear among the hearts of many believers—the prospect of personal rejection. "Given that more than 80 million adults contend that being on the receiving end of an evangelistic pitch is 'annoying' and knowing that several million born-again Christians refuse to describe themselves as born again for fear of becoming social outcasts, many churches and Christians have chosen to 'soft-sell' the gospel."[1] Sadly a disturbing number of churches have sold out to a "cheap-grace gospel" by attempting to water down the strong, accurate, and authoritative truth of the gospel. The outcome has been an increase in Christians keeping their faith to themselves. A growing majority of Christians, not just non-Christians, are opting for a nation that allows freedom of religion as long as it is exercised quietly, privately, and without public display.

What is the result of this silence? The world's greatest message is quickly becoming the world's greatest secret! Vast numbers of God's people, who have been commissioned to carry the gospel message throughout a spiritually dark world, have surrendered to political and social pressures brought on by the mainstream public to keep one's personal faith silent and private. Rather than subjecting themselves to possible rejection, exclusion, or ridicule for being an agent of spiritual influence, they have become *influenced* agents—intimidated by the very society that they are commissioned to transform with the message of redemption.

Truths about Fear

It's ironic when you think about it. Most Christians have a long list of reasons why they cannot talk to someone about Jesus, and most unbelievers have a long list of excuses why they cannot listen to someone share the gospel. Somewhere behind the pretext of both lies the element of fear that hinders one from sharing and one from receiving the gospel. Allow me to share some important truths concerning the fear of rejection.

Not All Fear Is Bad

A certain degree of fear is normal for most, and even helpful at times. Fear helps to keep us on our toes; we become more alert, aware, and in tune with our audience or surroundings. Have you ever walked into a dark room that you've never been in before? What happens to your fear factor? Perhaps more important, what happens to your alert factor? Your eyes are wide open, your ears attentive, and your hands and arms out in front of you for guidance and control. From a spiritual or evangelistic standpoint, fear can be good when it leads us to have a stronger confidence in God and less confidence in ourselves. Fear can also lead us to be in a more prayerful spirit that seeks God's blessing and involvement. Yet, when fear keeps us from witnessing, it becomes a hindrance.

Don't Allow Preconceived Notions of Rejection to Hinder You

I must admit that I'm terrible when it comes to this. Perhaps you do this as well. I will often expect an outcome before a witnessing encounter takes place. In other words, I prejudge the person I am about to witness to. Quite often, the result is nothing like I imagined in my mind. Such was the case not long ago when I made an evangelistic visit with a young couple. For several weeks the young couple had been attending our church. Each week I would see them at the close of the worship service and talk to them. The wife was always smiling, friendly, and full of conversation. The husband, on the other hand, was a little different. He was quiet and came across as standoffish and introverted.

We assigned this young couple to one of our REACH Teams. I followed up with that team captain and asked, "How is the relationship building going with the new prospective couple?" The response was, "Well, pastor, to be honest, not so good." "What's the problem?" I inquired. "Well, to tell you the truth, the wife is really friendly. She wants to get involved in some of our fellowship and activity requests. However, I don't think the husband likes us much."

I decided to make a personal pastoral visit to their home. I set up an appointment and drove over to their home one evening. All the way there, I perceived in my mind how the husband would react. First, I imagined him completely zoning out and not listening to a word I would say. Then I imagined that he would erupt suddenly and demand that I leave their home immediately. By the time I got to their doorstep, I was experiencing all kinds of fear.

The husband came to the door and said, "Hi, Pastor Scott; come on in." So far the visit was going extremely well. I mean, after all, he didn't throw me off his front porch or sic an attack dog on me. We sat down in the living room area and began a casual conversation. Amazingly he was laughing and joking around, acting nothing at all as I had imagined. Finally I got the nerve to ask him an evangelistic exploratory question, "Dave, if you were to die tonight and stand before the Lord and he were to ask you, 'Why should I let you into my heavenly kingdom?' what would you say?" I wished I had worn my running shoes because I knew I would soon be headed for the door. Surprisingly he replied, "I don't think I would go to heaven if I died tonight, but I'd like to know how to get there." I couldn't believe it. I had convinced myself that he would be rude and insensitive to the gospel. Thankfully, such was not the case at all. That night the young husband confessed Jesus Christ as his Savior.

Most of our preconceived fears are completely unfounded. I've discovered that most unbelievers are open to talk about spiritual matters. Sometimes their facade or demeanor may send you a different signal, but don't give up on them too quickly. Remember, most people, if approached in a gentle, transparent manner, will react with respect, kindness, and sincere interest.

Fear Does Not Excuse Us from Our Responsibility to Witness

Even if people do respond in a less-than-positive manner, that is no excuse to walk away from our responsibility to be a witness for Christ. If we wait until our fear of rejection is gone, most of us will be waiting forever. We can either choose to let fear control us, or we can act in faith and allow God to use us for his glory. We do not have to be afraid when we know that God is with us in every witnessing encounter. Remember the promise we have in Hebrews 13:5–6: "God has said, 'Never will I leave you; never will I forsake you.' So we say with confidence, 'The Lord is my helper; I will not be afraid. What can man do to me?'"

Replace Your Fear with Power, Love, and Self-Discipline That Comes from God

Notice again 2 Timothy 1:7: "For God did not give us a spirit of timidity, but a spirit of power, of love and of self-discipline." Notice the word *power*. It is the Greek word *dynamis*, meaning "great force" or "miraculous strength." We must remember that God gives the power and strength to witness effectively. Boldness is God-given courage that overcomes fear and produces freedom in sharing the gospel.

Witnessing for Christ should always be exercised in the power of God, not in our own strength. It's okay if you feel a bit inadequate in your witness. God never intended for you to feel completely adequate within yourself when it comes to doing his work and will. The Bible tells us that his strength is made perfect through our weakness.

Think about the rugged outdoorsman Simon Peter. After the arrest of Jesus, Peter relied on his own strength and denied ever knowing Christ, even when questioned by a girl (Mark 14:66–70). However, after the Spirit of the Lord came upon him, he displayed incredible boldness and power (Acts 4:13–31; 5:28–29). How was Peter's boldness and power mustered? Acts 4 gives us three indicators of how boldness and power are produced: First, spiritual power is manifested through us when we spend time with Jesus in personal fellowship (v. 13). Second, supernatural power is made manifest in response to our prayers (vv. 29–31). Third, spiritual power is a by-product of the filling of the Holy Spirit within each of us (v. 31).

God has given us a spirit not only of power but also of love. Love should move us beyond our fear of rejection. In fact, 1 John 4:18 states, "perfect love drives out fear." A young student once asked Adrian Rogers, senior pastor of Bellvue Baptist Church in Memphis, Tennessee, for advice on how to lead a church in evangelistic outreach. Rogers replied, "Your zeal is never any greater than your conviction. You can cheer others with your enthusiasm or their loyalty to the church or put them on a guilt trip for a while, but the only thing that will have a lasting effect is their love of the Lord Jesus Christ. It's not even a love for souls that sends people out; it's the love of Jesus that sends people out."[2]

I hear people all the time say something like, "I love my friend too much to drive a wedge between us by witnessing to him." I respond, "How much do you really love that person?" I've discovered that most unsaved friends are actually encouraged and uplifted when a saved friend risks rejection in order to reveal the truth of the gospel. Remember, love is a verb; it shows action. Love causes us to do things that otherwise we would never consider doing. Love motivates us to move beyond our comfort zones to act for the benefit and support of another. Love provides passion, acceptance, forgiveness, and perseverance. Love is the most potent motivator in witnessing.

God has not only given us power and love but also self-discipline. Discipline overcomes the fear of failure. As we discipline ourselves to learn how to share the gospel, to spend time praying for the lost, and to spend time cultivating relationships with lost people, we will become more effective in our witness for Christ. Remember: An undisciplined life is an undeveloped life.

What Questions to Expect

Most people ask questions that fall into five different categories:[3]

1. Theological Questions

Most of us don't consider ourselves theologians. We don't have seminary or Bible college degrees. So how can the average Christian handle tough theological questions? Understand that at some point you will receive some tough questions dealing with theological issues. Jesus received numerous questions related to theological issues. So will you. Therefore, you must be willing to grow in your spiritual aptitude.

2. Ethical Questions

Christians today will likely be bombarded with some extremely tough ethical questions dealing with such issues as abortion, homosexuality, genetic engineering, capital punishment, and assisted suicide. You have to be prepared to give an answer, or else you run the risk of losing some sense of credibility in your faith and belief system.

3. Hypothetical Questions

There are always people who ask questions for argument's sake, not because they really desire an honest answer. These are usually people who like to "chase rabbits" in an attempt to create endless cycles of discussion. Inevitably someone will ask a question such as, "If God can do anything, can he create a rock so big that he cannot lift it?" Or perhaps the tried-and-true question of all time, "What did God make first, the chicken or the egg?" These types of questions often come across as ridiculous or idiotic and are usually unanswerable.

4. Philosophical Questions

These can be some of the most difficult questions to deal with. In our postmodern world, people are more astute in philosophical thought and reason. Admittedly most Christians shy away from the topic of philosophy, mostly because the mere thought of the word often conjures up ideas of hollow and deceptive human reason. But at its root, the word *philosopher* simply means "lover of wisdom" (from the Greek *philos* plus *sophia*). And since God desires that we too become lovers of wisdom (see the Old Testament books of Proverbs and Ecclesiastes), we need to pay close attention to the philosophical trends of our society.

5. Personal Questions

At some point in every person's life, one asks the question, "Why am I here?" Without question, people are searching for the answer to their individual significance and purpose in life. "Surely life must be more than going to work, paying bills, raising kids, paying taxes, and dying?" one asks. They want to know why they should bother to get out of bed and face another day. They want to know if God is real—and if he is, what difference can he make in their lives?

Dealing with Tough Questions

How do you deal with tough questions when asked? Let me offer you the following words of advice.

Become a Student of the Word of God

Paul counseled young Timothy, "Do your best to present yourself to God as one approved, a workman who does not need to be ashamed and who correctly handles the word of truth" (2 Tim. 2:15). One of the reasons Christians fear witnessing is that they might be asked a question they cannot answer.

Most people in our society have adopted a postmodernism belief system. During the Modern Age, the vast majority of people assumed rational knowledge was absolute, certain, and good. Modernists assumed that science and education would

190

lead to a more productive society, and in the process solve many of humanity's ills. Postmodernists, however, have become disillusioned by science and education. Postmodernists are now under the basic assumption that all truth is relative. Often they are more interested in emotion and intuition than in logic and absolute truth. Over a decade ago, Andres Tapia was on target when he assessed that eighty-one percent of Generation Xers do not believe in absolute truth.[4]

This is why Christians need to be educated, trained, and strengthened in their faith. Every Christian ought to be a part of a regular Bible study or small group fellowship that spends ample time in God's Word. Second, every Christian should have a daily quiet time with the Lord. Perhaps never before in all recorded history do we live in an age with such an abundance of spiritual books, programs, and study aids, yet suffer from such biblical illiteracy in our churches. Third, begin keeping a spiritual journal. I'm not talking about a daily diary. I'm talking about recording the important insights and understandings that the Lord reveals to you each day. In the process, you can monitor your continued growth and maturation in the Lord.

Possess a Keen Awareness of Your Audience

Paul utilized this strategy when he spoke to the people at Mars Hill (Acts 17:16–34). Athens was the cultural and educational center of the world at that time. It was also a city full of shrines, temples, and altars signifying a variety of gods. This troubled Paul deeply. Therefore, he analyzed his audience before he actually spoke to them. He thought through his words carefully and with precision. Paul recognized that his audience was largely ignorant—not of religious matters but of spiritual matters. They really didn't know any better. He stood before them and said, "Men of Athens! I see that in every way you are very religious. For as I walked around and looked carefully at your objects of worship, I even found an altar with the inscription: 'TO AN UNKNOWN GOD.' Now what you worship as something unknown I am going to proclaim to you" (Acts 17:22–23). He recognized the need of his audience and sought to meet that need with respect and honor. In essence, he built a bridge. Become a friend, a listener, someone who makes an authentic effort toward understanding.

Don't Answer What You Don't Know

It is okay to respond to a person's query with "I don't know the answer to that question." I've been a pastor now for more than twenty years. I have earned masters and doctoral degrees from a highly accredited seminary. I've been a student of the Bible for twenty-five years. Yet still at times I have to tell people I don't have the answer to their question. I discovered a long time ago that it is far worse to offer a wrong answer to someone's inquiry and give the impression you know what you're talking about than to simply to tell the person, "I don't know the answer to your question, but if you will allow me time, I will get the answer for you." In most cases, people are more than willing to allow you time for research and study. Don't ever be forced into an answer that you're unsure about. Remember, a person's soul is at stake. You are dealing with eternal matters of dire importance. If you don't have an immediate answer, take the time to find it, both for the sake of your testimony and the person's inquiry.

Don't Get Pulled into Foolish Arguments

I think it would be safe to say that few have ever been argued into the kingdom of heaven. When the woman at the well attempted to draw Jesus into an argument over the religious and societal differences that existed between the Jews and Samaritans, he refused to engage her appeal. Instead of entertaining fruitless discourse, Jesus brought her back to the main message. Certainly there are grounds for disagreement. You should make every effort to make your point clear and precise. At the same time, however, we cannot afford to lose focus on our primary objective. The goal is not to win an argument but to lead a lost soul to faith (2 Tim. 2:23–26).

Always Apply Tact and Respect

I read about a barber who, as a new believer, attended a meeting where the guest speaker stressed the importance of sharing one's faith. The barber knew he was lacking in this area of his newfound faith, so he decided that he would take the first opportunity that came along that day. Sure enough, a first-time customer came into the barbershop for a haircut. After the customer had been seated, and the apron was tucked around his neck, the barber began to strop his razor vigorously. Testing the edge, he turned to the man in the barber chair and blurted out, "Friend, are you ready to die and meet God?" The man looked at the razor and leaped quickly out of the chair and out the door! The barber had the right motive; he just needed to use a little more tact.

Philip displayed his tact effectively as he confronted the searching man from Ethiopia. Philip inquired of him, "Do you understand what you are reading?" Notice that he didn't attempt to browbeat, ridicule, or embarrass the Ethiopian. Instead he reached out with kindness and respect. As a result the Ethiopian invited Philip to join him in his chariot and share his insights on the passage of Scripture. What was the outcome? The Ethiopian was converted to Christ.

Paul offers a clear summation of how we should attempt to treat unbelievers:

> To the Jews I became like a Jew, to win the Jews. To those under the law I became like one under the law (though I myself am not under the law), so to win those under the law. To those not having the law I became like one not having the law (though I am not free from God's law but am under

Christ's law), so as to win those not having the law. To the weak I became weak, to win the weak. I have become all things to all men so that by all possible means I might save some. I do this for the sake of the gospel that I may share in its blessings.

1 Corinthians 9:20–23

A wise Christian told me years ago "to be careful not to bruise the fruit." We need to ask God to give us sensitive spirits to whomever we may engage in a spiritual conversation. If you know the person well, focus on their felt needs. If you don't know them well, be sensitive and listen. Don't be too quick to judge or make false assumptions. When you listen with respect and attention, you will discover that they will treat you with the same respect.

Inevitably you will be faced with unbelievers who offer excuses and objections to the gospel. Don't let an excuse keep you from sharing your faith. An excuse is nothing more than the skin of the truth wrapped around a lie. There are hundreds of objections that unbelievers attempt to use:[5]

"There are too many hypocrites in the church."

"If God is so loving, why does he allow evil to exist in the world?"

"Aren't we all going to heaven, just by different routes?"

"How can a loving God send someone to hell?"

In all likelihood, at the very core of one's objection lies the primary reason why people reject Jesus Christ—many people simply do not want to change. A person may offer numerous excuses or objections, but inevitably, the most common reason for refusing Christ is due to the change that occurs when a person truly accepts Christ as Lord. Jesus actually spoke about this very issue (see John 3:19–21). Sinful men often desire to remain in darkness. They fear light because light reveals darkness (sin), and sin must be regarded as an offense before God, and therefore, shunned by a true believer. By his natural state, sinful man loves darkness. Therefore, his natural reaction is to reject light or change from darkness.

An old proverb states, "When you throw a rock into a pack of dogs, the one that barks the loudest is the one that has been hit." Usually, but not always, the one who offers the most excuses and objections is the one who is closest to making a decision for Christ. Don't be discouraged and taken off guard when someone offers an excuse or objection. Stand firm, be steadfast, and trust the Lord to speak through your witness.

15

The Payoff Involved

Reaching the Harvest, One Relationship at a Time

A few years ago Ken and Tammy Slagle visited our church. I greeted them after the worship service, and we had a delightful conversation. Within a few weeks, I had set up an appointment with them. Both were already believers and deeply committed in their faith. They sensed that the Lord was leading them to unite with our church as members. Ken mentioned that he had other family members who were also looking for a new church home and that he wanted to invite them to worship with us. I encouraged him to invite all of them to an upcoming service.

Ken mentioned that he had a younger brother, Tom, who grew up in the church but had never made a profession of faith in Jesus. The entire Slagle family had been praying for Tom for several years. Tom had walked away from all involvement in church. Ken was hoping that I could meet him and establish a friendship. I suggested that he and Tom both participate in our annual men's ministry golf tournament.

Ken brought Tom as his playing partner. I walked over to them and introduced myself to Tom. He looked at me and said, "You're the preacher and you play golf?" "As much as my wife will let me," I replied. Tom couldn't believe that I played golf. (I think he was also surprised to see me in shorts and a polo shirt and not in a suit, tie, and wing tips!) We engaged in a casual conversation until the tournament began. Several of the other men in our church introduced themselves to him.

We completed the tournament and everyone gathered for a luncheon and award presentation. It just so happened that my partner and I won first place. (Don't be too impressed; this is the only golf tournament I've ever won, and probably the last!) After the trophies were handed out and people were leaving, Ken and Tom walked up to congratulate me. Tom said, "Scott, if you preach anything like you golf, I want to come to your church." I replied, "Tom, I would love for you and your family to attend one of our worship services, but please don't compare my preaching to my golfing!" We laughed and joked around for a while longer. As we began to depart, I said to Tom, "Hey, I really do hope that you and your family will join us tomorrow for worship." "I think we'll be there," he replied, with a hint of personal satisfaction that I had taken the time personally to invite him to come.

The next morning, Tom, his wife, Kim, and their two teen-age children were in attendance. During our welcome time in our worship, I made a direct beeline to Tom and said, "Hey, Tom, you made it! Thanks so much for being here today." He introduced me to his family as others in our church greeted them. After the service I met them at the door and told them how much I appreciated their visit with us. Tom said, "Pastor Scott, I really like what you do here at Fall Creek. The people here are really friendly and make you feel welcome."

Over the next several weeks, the Slagles continued to wor-ship regularly and even began attending a couple's Bible study class. More and more people within our church began to befriend them, extending fellowship and kindness. We also assigned a REACH Team to Tom and Kim, and those families began to establish meaningful relationships with them by inviting them to dinners, fellowships, and recreational activities.

I scheduled a pastoral visit with Tom and Kim one evening to talk to them about church membership, and specifically with Tom concerning his salvation. After several minutes of friendly conversation, I asked Tom if he had ever made a personal commitment of his life to Jesus Christ. He said, "I've thought about it most of my life, but I just haven't come to the point of making that decision." I replied, "Tom, is there any specific reason why you have never accepted Jesus Christ?" "Nobody has ever come right out and asked me that until now. I know I need to soon." I said, "What about right now?" "Right now?" Tom said with a look of surprise. "Sure, you don't need to be in the church to receive Christ. You can pray and receive him right now." I could sense that Tom had a sense of relief when I told him he could receive Jesus right there in his own living room. Tom did pray to receive Jesus that night. The following Sunday, Tom's family united with our church, and Tom made his public profession of faith in Christ.

The reason I tell this story is not because it is unique. I want you to see the vast number of people who played a significant role in Tom's decision for Christ.

- Tom's parents had been praying for him for several years.
- Tom's siblings had witnessed and prayed for him during that same time period.
- Tom's brother, Ken, made a specific effort to connect Tom to our church through the golf outing.
- Members of our church made Tom feel very welcome when he attended our church.

- One of our couple's Bible study classes reached out to Tom with acts of kindness and fellowship.
- One of our REACH Teams was immediately assigned to Tom and his family and began cultivating an evangelistic relationship.
- I befriended Tom and developed a meaningful relationship.

Every relationship was vital to his coming to Christ. The friendliness and attention that was demonstrated had a direct bearing on Tom's heart and life. Please don't get me wrong. Without question, conversion is the work of the Holy Spirit (see John 6:44; 1 Cor. 3:5–8). Only God can bring a true conversion. However, we are called of God to do the witnessing. He desires to work through us as his committed followers.

God works through us as we strive to establish meaningful relationships with those who are unsaved. And it takes all types of relationship-building efforts to accomplish the task of winning the lost. When I began to calculate in my mind how many people had either a direct or indirect bearing on Tom's conversion, I realized that hundreds of people had some type of impact. True, not every person presented the gospel message. However, everyone was used in some way to demonstrate the life-changing power and presence of the gospel.

If we are to reach our world with the message of the gospel, I don't think filling up stadiums and coliseums repeatedly with lost people and presenting the gospel is the primary method. In fact, a survey from the Institute of American Church Growth revealed that 75 to 90 percent of new believers come to Christ through a friend or acquaintance who takes time to present the gospel to them one-on-one. Interestingly only 17 percent of all conversions occur through what is called an "event"—a pastor preaching his Sunday morning message, a mass-crusade effort, or some type of high-attendance campaign.[1] With this in mind, what are some keys to establishing meaningful evangelistic relationships with unsaved people?

Begin Establishing Relationships with Unsaved People

The first place to begin is to assess where you are right now in your relationships with unsaved people. Do you currently know anyone with whom you can identify as being unsaved? Begin with your personal circle of influence (see appendix 2). Identify people whom you frequently come into contact with who are unsaved. Start with your immediate family and work outward based upon the degree of personal relationship you have with others. Also, do not be too quick to judge or write off someone at this point. For instance, just because a person tells you that they believe in God or attend a church is no guarantee that the person is truly saved. One of the keys to look for is authentic spiritual fruit in that person's life. If that person says they have a relationship with God, does the person's actions or lifestyle support the claim? Jesus warns that not everyone who claims to belong to God actually does (Matt. 7:16–18).

Begin to Take Your Relationship to the Next Level of Evangelistic Outreach

Once you have established a relationship with an unsaved person, you may ask, "How do I build an evangelistic relationship with this person?" Begin by defining the three basic levels of relationships.[2] The first is *A* level: *acquaintance relationship*. At this level you know the person's name, perhaps what they do for a living, and other surface facts about the person. To achieve this level takes little time, little investment of energy, and provides little to no return. The actual moment when you can share the gospel may not come until weeks or months later—after a more established friendship has developed.

The second relationship level is *B* level: *brotherly relationship*. Here you not only know the person's name and what they do for a living but you know their interests, enjoyments, and some of their plans for the future. At this level you have learned to appreciate one another's company and conversation. You seek to get together for fellowship and social interaction often. This level requires moderate time and energy and provides warm friendships at a casual level. This level provides for initial inquiry into spiritual matters; however, remember that key relational elements such as trust, transparency, and honesty need to be established.

The third relationship level is *C* level: *close relationship*. This is where real depth and intimacy occur. The level goes beyond the *who* and *what* to the deeper level of *why*—going underneath the surface to discover why they think and feel the way they do. This level has attained key ingredients of a successful relationship: loyalty, honesty, commitment, respect, transparency, and trust. The personal and spiritual rewards are priceless and immeasurable at this level. Understand that all relationships take time to develop and mature. Also realize that at any point in the relationship-building process the Holy Spirit may intervene to give you an opportunity to lead the person to Christ. Be sensitive to the person and to the Holy Spirit.

Ask God to Help You Get to Know Others Better

Make sure you remember names, and be sure to pronounce them correctly. People are genuinely impressed when you remember their names and backgrounds. As a pastor, I always try my best to remember the names of our unchurched visitors and guests on Sunday mornings. "Hey, you remembered my name." That means a lot to people. Take the time in conversation to ask people about themselves, then seek to remember their interests, families, and prayer needs in future communication. As they feel you are interested in them and seek to know them better, they are more likely to open up to you.

Smile and Be Friendly at All Times

Be the kind of person those around you want to associate with. If you desire to build lasting relationships, be kind, compassionate, and friendly at all times. *Note*: The person with whom you are establishing an evangelistic relationship may not always be friendly. You must love and accept them regardless of their disposition. Evangelistic relationships are not built exclusively with unsaved people who are like-minded or naturally appealing to us. We have to be willing to step out of our comfort zones to love the unlovely and befriend the unfriendly.

I often wonder if Jesus were on the earth today in a physical sense, with whom would he hang out? Would it be the preachers, missionaries, or evangelists? I don't think so. I've got the feeling that Jesus would probably hang out with "irregular people." You know who I'm talking about: the person at work whom no one invites to lunch, the person at the fitness center who works out alone, the person to whom no one talks at a social function. Irregular people are all around us. I also think Jesus would hang out at the prisons, jails, and juvenile centers. He would probably visit the AIDS clinics, cancer centers, and homeless shelters. In other words, the kind of people whom many of us forget about. Jesus could have hung out with the religious crowd, or only with the Jews. If he had, he would have saved himself a lot of ridicule and harassment. But he chose to make social sacrifices for the sake of outcasts, unacceptables, and irregulars.

Treat Others as You Would Have Them Treat You

One good rule of thumb is to treat others the way in which you would like to be treated in return. Three words come to mind when I think of how I would like for others to treat me—*courteous, caring,* and *complimentary*. Courteousness is a behavior that shows respect one for another. Caring is a feeling that demonstrates sensitivity and compassion for one another. Complimentary is the use of words that show support, favor, and encouragement. If you will treat others with these basic relational skills, they will treat you with the same respect and favor, and through the process, you will win a friend for life, not to mention a soul for eternity.

Learn to Be a Good Listener

Take time to discover the interests of others. Dale Carnegie once wrote, "You can make more friends in two months by becoming interested in other people than you can in two years by trying to get other people interested in you."[3] Perhaps you've heard the old adage, "Many persons call a doctor when all they really want is an audience." How true this is. So if you aspire to develop evangelistic relationships, be an attentive listener.

Always Be Willing to Take the Initiative to Help When Appropriate

If your new friend is going out of town for the week, offer to check his mail or take care of his pets. If he is going to paint his house, offer to grab a paintbrush and help. Also, be sensitive to the unsaved around you who may be hurting. Life is full of hurts, disappointments, and trials. Sickness, death of a loved one, marital disharmonies, financial pressures, and a host of other things can provide Christians with divine opportunities to share a clear witness by caring for, sharing with, and serving others. Keep in mind, people don't care how much you know until they know how much you care. The hurts of others can be God's opportunities for you to share his love. Availability is a great asset in establishing evangelistic relationships.

Allow Your Home to Be a Lighthouse for the Gospel to Shine

Opening your home to guests is a wonderful way of establishing hospitality and friendship. Meals are a great way to begin. Have you noticed in the Bible how often Jesus's ministry was centered on others partaking of a meal together? The Pharisees asked Jesus's disciples, "Why do you eat and drink with tax-collectors and 'sinners'?" (Luke 5:30). When was the last time you intentionally set out to invite an unsaved person over to your home for a meal?

Seek to Discover and Develop Common Interests

Your goal should be to discover some common interests that you share with your unsaved friends and cultivate the relationship through those activities. These shared common interests are often referred to as "contact points," things that can draw you together with another person, whereby helping to cultivate and solidify an ongoing relationship. Discovering a person's interest is as easy as asking, "What are some things you like to do in your spare time?"

Concentrate on Being Yourself

Sometimes when we get around people we don't know well, we try too hard to impress them. Just be you. Relax, be easygoing, and have fun. Don't feel like you have to say something "spiritual" the first time you have fellowship together. Often we think that if we have not shared our faith before the evening is concluded, we have failed in our witness. Such is not the case. It usually takes time to cultivate a relationship to the point where their hearts are ready to hear and receive the gospel. Breaking the ice on spiritual matters is important, but it should happen naturally, not come across as orchestrated or rehearsed.

Become a Giving Person

One of the keys to any meaningful relationship is giving and sacrifice. Show the unsaved person that you truly care for them as a person. Give of your time, talents, and treasures to show the unsaved person that you care for them. A good way to demonstrate a giving spirit and open up a witnessing opportunity is to give them a Christian resource (i.e., a Christian book, CD, or magazine). Offer to take them to a local Christian concert in your area. These activities can be creative avenues of presenting the gospel message of Jesus Christ.

Always Make Time for Others

Have you ever wished you had more hours in a day? Do you feel as if you have more things to accomplish in a day than time to accomplish them all? With this in mind, have you ever said, "I'd witness more if I just had more time." The fact is, we don't need more time. I firmly believe God gives us enough time in each day to accomplish everything "he wants us to do." Actually, we never "find" time to do something; we "make" time to do something. In other words, we prioritize our time and schedule wisely. What we must remember is that time is not our own; it is a stewardship God has entrusted to each of us. In light of that, we are to prioritize our time based upon God's desires, not ours. God's plan for our lives is more than mere existence. If God's only purpose in creating us was to save us, then why doesn't he immediately transport us to heaven at the moment of conversion? The reality is that God has a greater purpose for us.

Most people struggle with time management. How do we make time to be effective witnesses for God? First, *learn to distinguish between time makers and time wasters.* Americans waste a tremendous amount of time doing things that amount to little value. What is the greatest time waster? Without question, our greatest robber of time is the television. In 1991 the *Chicago Tribune* reported the results of a survey that focused on the television-viewing habits of Americans. The *Tribune* survey concluded that the average American spends approximately thirty hours per week watching television.[4] Over a fifty-year period, this totals seventy-eight thousand hours, or almost nine years of one's life! Wouldn't we become better stewards of our time if we cut down on our TV viewing and spent that time investing in the lives of others?

Second, *manage your time wisely by keeping a schedule.* I've discovered that keeping a time schedule actually helps me to "make" time for people rather than scrambling around trying to "find" time for others. A schedule does not have to be etched in stone; it can always be adjusted when needs develop. But without a schedule, we are left open to any abrupt change that occurs. Make people a priority on your calendar.

Third, *use your time creatively.* One of the great things about the REACH Team concept is that you can spend time in fellowship with believers and nonbelievers at the same time. You can also spend time with your family. For instance, schedule an outing to a baseball game or a concert in the community. The possibilities are endless if we will only allow time to work to our advantage.

Always Practice Patience, Tenderness, and Kindness

By nature, most of us tend to be impatient. Perhaps it is because we live in the age of "instant gratification." Automatic coffeemakers, express lanes in supermarkets, and drive-through lanes at restaurants. I must admit, I'm very impatient. I tend to get fidgety when the person ahead of me in the "ten items or less" aisle at the grocery has eleven or more items! (That's right; I count their items.)

For these reasons, when God tells me to be patient when it comes to sharing my faith, it is not always easy for me. Sometimes the seeds we sow today may not take root for weeks, months, even years. This is often true when it comes to our unsaved family members. I've known members of my churches who have prayed and witnessed to their unsaved family members for years, only to find themselves waiting for the harvest to come. Some have even given up on the harvest. I'm so glad that the Slagle family didn't give up on their son and brother, Tom. Aren't you glad somebody didn't give up on you? So be patient. Be willing to wait. Remember, God is sovereign. Trust your unsaved family member or friend to Jesus Christ and wait patiently for the harvest to come. "Let us not become weary in doing good, for at the proper time we will reap a harvest if we do not give up" (Gal. 6:9).

Leave the Timing in God's Hands

We must be sensitive to the timing and leading of the Holy Spirit. As Scripture reminds us, we must "be prepared in season and out of season" (2 Tim. 4:2). Perhaps another way of saying that is "Be on duty at all times." One of the clearest examples of this is found in Acts 8:26–38. Here we read the story of Philip, who was enjoying a successful ministry in Samaria when he was instructed to go down to the desert. When he arrived, he was led to a man in a chariot who was the treasurer for the queen of Ethiopia—a man of great importance and wealth. The man was searching for meaning in life. His search led him to Jerusalem, the spiritual capital of the world. While there, he secured a copy of Isaiah's writings.

Philip came alongside this man's chariot and found the man reading Isaiah's work. It just so happened that Philip found himself in the right place at the right time. Because he was willing and ready, Philip had the opportunity to lead that man to faith in Jesus Christ.

Building evangelistic relationships means that we must plan to share Christ intentionally yet be ready and willing to respond spontaneously at any given time. The Holy Spirit allows us to observe others in need and be sensitive to them. And we show our love by serving and befriending them. We must demonstrate the message of the gospel to those who are searching and in despair. "We loved you so much that we were delighted to share with you not only the gospel of God but our lives as well, because you had become so dear to us" (1 Thess. 2:8).

Epilogue

It's Worth the Investment

Nothing is more thrilling than seeing new people enter into the church family as a result of evangelistic and outreach efforts. Such was the case for Alan and Robin Oglesby, along with their two precious children, Rachel and Jack. The following story illustrates that evangelistic relationship building with the unchurched is worth our investment of time, energy, and effort. Alan writes:

> My wife, Robin, and I, after seven years at a small church that we loved, found ourselves searching for a new church home. Although we both have been Christians since our early childhood, our experience at this church taught us the value of service and true fellowship with a church family.
>
> It was not easy starting over again. Our first priority in a church was that it be fundamentally sound and grounded in the Scriptures. However, we also knew that we would not be happy or feel a sense of belonging if we were not able to plug in, especially with personal friendships with others toward whom we enjoyed a common bond.
>
> On the first Sunday we visited Fall Creek Baptist Church, we were invited to lunch—great start! With each passing week

211

that we visited, we were invited to people's homes, to weekday lunches, weekly Bible studies, and a picnic with a small group of families. It proved to be an extraordinary, friendly place. There was also a sense of accountability in that people noticed and followed up with us out of sincere interest, especially if we happened to miss a service on successive occasions.

The REACH Team ministry was greatly instrumental in our family's decision to make Fall Creek our new church home. We felt a connection to the families who "REACHed" out to us. We wanted to worship and serve alongside these people who had become our friends. It is now approximately one year since we joined Fall Creek, and we continue to serve in several areas of our new church home, including becoming team members on a REACH Team.

It was not by accident, coincidence, or happenstance that the Oglesbys united with our church. From the time of their first visit, they were embraced as friends, not shunned as strangers or newcomers. In essence, they were loved into our church. REACH Team members intentionally went out of their way as a unified team to show the love and grace of Jesus Christ. It was intentional, relational, and hospitable evangelism displayed by genuine, authentic Christians. I am absolutely convinced that more people would not only visit our churches but would profess faith in Christ and unite with our churches if we, the body of Christ, simply went out of our way to "love" more people into the church.

I'm reminded of a story I once read to my daughter, Hollie Beth, when she was just a little girl. *The Velveteen Rabbit* is a story about a group of toys that live in a nursery. Two of the main characters in the book, Rabbit and the Skin Horse, have an open conversation about what it means to be "real." The Skin Horse tells the Rabbit that being real is not based upon how you are made. Rather, when a child loves you for a long, long time, not just to play with, but really loves you, then you become real. The Skin Horse went on to say that toys that break easily, have sharp edges, or have to be carefully kept usually don't become real. "It's the toys that have all their hair loved and rubbed off and their eyes pulled out that become the most real."[1]

In closing out this final section, I want to challenge you, the reader, to become real with others. This is what twenty-first-century evangelism is all about—being real and relational with the unchurched. Becoming real in *The Velveteen Rabbit* doesn't happen to toys that break easily, have sharp edges, or have to be carefully guarded. Becoming real in the Christian community means that we must become people who don't break easily, have sharp edges, or have to carefully guard ourselves against others. Simply stated, we have to be willing to expose ourselves to potential hurts, letdowns, and rejections in order to love those outside the church. It calls for our sacrifice, humility, and openness.

This was exactly what Jesus did. He made sacrifice after sacrifice in order to demonstrate his love for all people—Jew or Gentile, rich or poor, educated or illiterate. He, the great Sovereign of the entire universe, humbled himself as a man and mixed freely with the commoners, the outcasts, and even the sick and afflicted. Ultimately he opened himself up completely, allowing others to see the very nature of God so that they might know the Father's unconditional love and acceptance. We too must run the risk of becoming real through our relationships and acts of hospitality so that the unchurched might see and experience the love of God that is found in Jesus Christ.

I challenge you to open yourself up to a world of people all around you who need God's love. Let me encourage you to take some risks for God. Will some people reject your acts of hospitality? Yes. Will some people ridicule you for being kind and considerate? Perhaps. Will some people laugh at you and label you as a fanatic for sharing your faith? Most likely. But remember what Jesus said, "If the world hates you, keep in mind that it hated me first" (John 15:18). Love people as Jesus loves others and start loving them by establishing meaningful relationships through acts of hospitality and kindness.

REACH Team Participant's Guide

Lesson 1
Introduction
"What Is REACH Team?"

NOTES

(Read introduction of *REACH*.)

REACH Team is an _evangelistic_ and
assimilating strategy that targets the unchurched through _relationship_ -building
principles and personal acts of _hospitality_.
The word *REACH* is an acronym that
means:

R: _relational_
E: _evangelism_
A: _and_
C: _relational_
H: _ospitality_

3 Types of Evangelism

* Intentional / Confrontational
• Relational / friendship
° Servant / Acts of Hospitality

T: together
E: everyone
A: accomplishes
215 M: more

Luke 10:1-2

NOTES

Let's take a closer look at each of these words:

Relational

1. People in our society are looking for meaningful and purposeful *relationships*
2. The goal for our church is to *build* relationships that last with the unchurched.
3. Our church is needing people who are willing to *participate* in building meaningful relationships with the unchurched.

Key Verse "Love the Lord your God with all of your heart, and with all of your soul, and with all of your mind. This is the first and greatest commandment. And the second is like it: Love your neighbor as yourself" (Matt. 22:37–39).

Evangelism

1. The mandate for any church is to go and *tell* the Good News of Jesus Christ.

Key Verse "Go therefore and make disciples of all nations, baptizing them in the name of the Father, and of the Son, and of the Holy Spirit, teaching them to obey everything I have commanded you. And surely I am with you always, to the very end of the age" (Matt. 28:19–20).

2. The goal for our church is to *train* adequately all REACH Team participants to share their faith in a *simple* and effective manner.

216

3. The REACH Team strategy makes evangelism efforts both _personal_ and _relational_.

NOTES

And

1. The word _and_ represents more than just a conjunction that connects words or phrases. It denotes the _how to_ concerning the efforts and actions of relational evangelism.

2. The REACH Team strategy attempts to train people how to share their faith in a _variety_ of ways.

Key Verse "Do not cause anybody to stumble, whether Jews, Greeks or the church of God—even as I try to please everybody in every way. For I am not seeking my own good but the good of many, so that they may be saved" (1 Cor. 10:33).

3. The goal for our church is for the unchurched to come away with a more _positive_ _attitude_ of Christianity and the church as a result of our relationships and acts of hospitality.

Cultivational

1. One of the keys to the REACH Team strategy is in the _developing_ or cultivating of evangelistic prospects.

Key Verse "I tell you, open your eyes and look at the fields! They are ripe for harvest" (John 4:35).

2. The REACH Team strategy teaches believers how to establish and develop _meaningful_ and lasting relationships with the unchurched.

217

NOTES   *Hospitality*

1. In today's society, many unchurched people are guarded in their personal lives, thereby refusing Christians the opportunity to make <u>Cold Call</u> evangelistic visits.

2. People today are looking for <u>authentic</u>, genuine relationships. Because of this, the unchurched community is looking closely at Christians to see if the <u>faith</u> they proclaim is <u>real</u>.

3. Another key in the implementation of the REACH Team strategy is for ministry <u>participants</u> to cultivate evangelistic relationships with the unchurched by demonstrating <u>acts</u> of kindness and hospitality.

Key Verse "Above all, love each other deeply because love covers a multitude of sins. Offer <u>hospita</u>lity to one another" (1 Pet. 4:8–9).

Lesson 2
What Are the Expectations for Participating in REACH Team?

(Read chaps. 1, 2, 5, and 6 of *REACH.*)

As a REACH Team participant, you are expected to do the following:

1. Read carefully the book <u>REACH</u> and apply its basic principles and instructions.

2. Attend a REACH Team <u>training</u> <u>seminar</u> sponsored by your church.

3. Work with and support the <u>team</u> you are assigned to, making every effort to <u>encourage</u> one another toward good works.

218

4. Strive daily to be a vital _witness_
to the unchurched people assigned to your
team (visitation prospects), and those around
you (your circle of influence) by developing
evangelistic _relationships_ through your personal and corporate acts of hospitality.

5. Commit to attend the monthly
REACH Team _celebration_ rallies that
serve to motivate, encourage, and inform
all participants.

6. Have _fun_! Being a witness
for Christ should be a daily experience
for all Christians, therefore, make it a
joyful event in your life.

What is _not_ expected of you through
your participation in REACH Team?

1. You are not required to _memorize_
lengthy outlines or "canned" approaches to
personal evangelism.

2. You are not required to attend
weekly training meetings, or scheduled visitation efforts.

3. You are not required to make "cold-
call" _impromptu visits_ to people you do not
know, whereby feeling _pressured_ to produce an immediate evangelistic outcome.

NOTES

Lesson 3
Understanding the Team Concept for Evangelistic Outreach

(Read chaps. 2, 9, and 13 of _REACH_.)

By creating REACH Teams, these small
groups work to develop and cultivate

NOTES _friendships_ with unchurched prospects
through relationship-building activities
and _intentional_ acts of hospitality. What
are some advantages to the REACH Team
evangelism approach?

1. The small group setting is non
   threatening to most unchurched
   people.
2. No special _facilities_ are required.
3. The casual atmosphere of a small
   group provides an _attractive_
   atmosphere.
4. The small group provides
   intimacy
5. The personal interaction of a small
   group allows for people to find
   answers to their questions
   easier.
6. Small groups offer _flexible_
   scheduling for events and activities.
7. Small groups provide a greater atmosphere to talk about _spiritual_
   matters.
8. Small groups provide a good
   foundation for those making
   decisions for Christ.

REACH Team Design

• Each REACH Team is designed to have
three families (or separate individuals)
from within the church who constitute a
team.

• Each REACH Team should have
one family (or individual) who is
recognized by the team as its designated
leader.

- Each REACH Team will cultivate **NOTES**
relationships with the unchurched
through three specific avenues:

(1) *assigned prospects who have visited the church*

(2) *personally established prospects from your circle of influence.*

(3) *personally established prospects from ~~celebrations~~ acts of hospitality.*

- Each REACH Team participant is *encouraged* to attend a monthly
REACH Team celebration meeting.

Lesson 4
Relationship-Building Principles

(Read chaps. 1, 10, and 15 of *REACH*.)

Building relationships with the unchurched is the key to *reaching* others
with the gospel message of Jesus Christ.
The REACH Team approach to relationship building focuses on three areas:

1. With *prospects* who have been
assigned to your team for group
cultivation.

Keys to Remember

- An *initial* contact needs to be
made by a group member within the
first twenty-four hours after the prospect has visited your church.

221

NOTES

- Make sure that someone from your team personally _invites_ the prospect back to church the following Sunday.
- Involve the prospect in some type of team group _activity_ as soon as possible in order to begin establishing relationships.
- Follow up _frequently_ through personal phone calls, emails, notes, or visits. A week should not go by without someone from the team making a personal contact with the assigned prospect.

2. With prospects developed through your personal circle of influence (see appendix 2, "My Circle of Influence").

Defining Your Circle of Influence

1. _immediate family_
2. _extended family_
3. _close friends_
4. _neighbors/social acquaintances_
5. _business/school acquaintances_
6. _other acquaintances_

3. With prospects developed as a result of reaching out through acts of _hospitality_.

Keys to Consider When Performing Acts of Hospitality in Your Local Community

1. Determine the _project/idea_ that works best for your REACH Team and the local community.

222

NOTES

2. Plan to perform one community act of hospitality every ~~about~~ 8 to ~~about~~ 12 weeks.
3. Don't be afraid of *spontaneous* opportunities.
4. Each act of hospitality project should have a specific *time frame* for implementation.
5. Each REACH Team will probably have to provide some *funding* for needed supplies when conducting acts of hospitality projects.
6. Be aware of *needs* that exist in your local area.
7. Always report your *results* to your REACH Team director/coordinator.

Keys to Becoming More "People Centered" in Your Evangelism Efforts

1. Always be *patient* with the unchurched.
2. Learn to become more *sensitive* to the needs of the unchurched around you.
3. Seek to love the unchurched *unconditionally*
4. Make time in your busy schedule to meet the needs of the unchurched through *random* acts of hospitality.
5. Be genuine in your actions knowing that the unchurched world is always *watching*.
6. Be a *friend* first, but with the heart of an evangelist.

NOTES   *Three Stages of Relationships*

1. Level A: _Acquaintance_ relationship
2. Level B: _Brotherly_ relationship
3. Level C: _Close_ relationship

Lesson 5
Learning to Pray for the Unchurched

(Read chap. 12 of *REACH.*)

Keys to Praying for Lost and Unchurched People

1. Establish a prayer _list_ of
   people you know who are unsaved.
2. Ask God to _give_ you unsaved
   people to pray for.
3. Pray that God will give you
   opportunities to share your faith.
4. Stay _confessed up_ and clean from
   all sin.
5. Pray for _supernatural boldness_
   to share your faith.
6. Pray that Christ will be _reflected_
   through your life each day.
7. Pray that God will fill you daily with
   his _love_ and _grace_.
8. Pray for more _laborers_ to go
   into the harvest fields.
9. Pray that God will bring a genuine
   sense of personal _conviction_ to the
   heart of the unsaved person you are
   praying for.
10. Always pray for the unsaved person
    by _name_.

Lesson 6
Evangelism Sharing Strategy

NOTES

(Read chap. 11 of *REACH.*)

Reasons People Fail to Share Their Faith

1. "I'm not a good enough person to share my faith."
2. "I don't have the qualifications to share my faith."
3. "I'm afraid to share my faith."
4. "I don't feel like sharing my faith."

Three Keys to Developing Your Personal Testimony

1. Separation from Christ. (What you were like before Christ.)
2. Salvation through Christ. (What Christ has done for you.)
3. Security in Christ. (What you are like now in Christ.)

- Testimony should be 3-5 minutes long
- Memorize Romans 6:23
- The "Hand-Out" Presentation
- Gospel Tract

(Go to chap. 11 and write out your personal testimony.)

Note: Your seminar/conference leader may have you learn one or more of the gospel presentations that are provided in chapter 11. These are simple outlines that require little memorization. If your church chooses to utilize another gospel presentation, then omit this request and move on to the next lesson.

Lesson 7
Implementing the REACH Team

(Read chaps. 5–6 of *REACH.*)

NOTES

Monthly REACH Team Celebration Meetings

All REACH Team participants are *encouraged* to attend a monthly celebration meeting. The reason for participation is:

1. *Education*
2. *Motivation*
3. *Inspiration*
4. *Petition*
5. *Celebration*

Guidelines for Implementing Acts of Hospitality through Relational Evangelism

1. When appropriate, ask for *permission* to perform community acts of hospitality.
2. Make sure to have all of your *supplies* in advance.
3. Stick to your assigned *schedule* and time arrangements.
4. Practice *safety* at all times.
5. Demonstrating *kindness* is paramount.
6. Always do your very *best*.
7. *Review* and discuss the "pros" and "cons" of every social and community event.
8. Be in a spirit of *prayer* throughout the duration of your event.
9. Don't *worry* with the idea of seeing immediate results.
10. Please do not *charge* a fee for your community service.
11. Plan for *expenses* when providing a service to the community.

226

12. Have an _alternate_ project in re-
    serve in case of inclement weather.
13. Discover what community
    projects work best for your
    team.
14. As pastors, make sure to allow each
    team _permission_ to minister freely.
15. Don't let the fear of _mistakes_
    keep you from serving.

NOTES

Answer Key

All answers are in order of blanks within each lesson.

Lesson 1

evangelistic
assimilating
relationship
hospitality
relational
evangelism
and
cultivational
hospitality
relationships
build
participate
tell
train
simple
personal
relational
how-to
variety
positive attitude
developing
meaningful
cold-call
authentic
faith
real
participants
acts

Lesson 2

REACH
training seminar
team
encourage
witness

relationships
celebration
fun
joyful
memorize
weekly
impromptu visits
pressured

Lesson 3

friendships
intentional
threatening
facilities
attractive
intimacy
answers
flexible
spiritual
decisions
three
one
leader
assigned prospects
  who have visited
  the church
personally established
  prospects created
  through your
  circle of influence
personally established
  prospects as a
  result of commu-
  nity acts of
  hospitality
encouraged

Lesson 4

reaching
prospects
initial
invites
activity
frequently
immediate family
  members
extended family
  (relatives)
close friends
neighbors/social
  acquaintances
business/school
  acquaintances
other acquaintances
hospitality
project/idea
~~four~~ 8
~~eight~~ 2
spontaneous
time frame
funding
needs
results
patient
sensitive
unconditionally
random
watching
friend
Acquaintance
Brotherly
Close

228

Lesson 5

list
give
opportunities
"confessed up"
supernatural boldness
reflected
love
grace
laborers
conviction
name

Lesson 6

good
qualifications

afraid
feel
Separation
Salvation
Security

Lesson 7

encouraged
education
motivation
inspiration
petition
celebration
permission
supplies
schedule

safety
kindness
best
Review
prayer
worry
charge
expenses
alternate
projects
permission
mistakes

Appendix 2

My Circle of Influence

Keep a record of the unchurched in your *circle of influence* with whom you can cultivate evangelistic relationships.

**(1) Immediate Family
   Members**

_____

_____

_____

_____

_____

_____

**(2) Extended Family
   (Relatives)**

_____

_____

_____

_____

_____

_____

_____

(3) Close Friends

_____

_____

_____

_____

_____

_____

(4) Neighbors/Social Acquaintances

_____

_____

_____

_____

_____

_____

_____

(5) Business/School Acquaintances

_____

_____

_____

_____

_____

_____

(6) Other Acquaintances

_____

_____

_____

_____

_____

_____

Notes

Introduction

1. Bureau of the Census, *Statistical Abstracts of the United States 2000*, prepared by the Department of Commerce in cooperation with the Bureau of the Census (Washington, D.C., 2000).

2. This percentage is based upon research comprised by the Barna Research Group. The figure is based upon a series of national surveys among random samples of the adult population within the United States. In conducting these surveys, the Barna Group defined "Christian" as those who say they have made a personal commitment to Jesus Christ, and that the commitment is still relevant and personal in their lives today, and for those who believe that when they die they will go to heaven because they have confessed their sins and accepted Jesus Christ as their Savior. For a further discussion of this research, see George Barna, *Evangelism That Works* (Ventura, CA: Regal, 1994).

3. Bill Hybels and Mark Mittelberg, *Becoming a Contagious Christian* (Grand Rapids: Zondervan, 1994), 13.

4. Thom Rainer, *Surprising Insights from the Unchurched* (Grand Rapids: Zondervan, 2001), 41.

5. George Barna, "We Have Seen the Future: The Demise of Christianity in Los Angeles County" (Glendale, CA: Barna Research Group, 1990).

6. George Barna, *Growing Your Church from the Outside In* (Ventura, CA: Regal, 2002), 24.

7. Ibid.

233

Chapter 1: The Relational Approach to Evangelism

1. Rainer, *Surprising Insights*, 72. Rainer's research was based upon surveys performed on the previously unchurched who had connected with a local church. The survey also indicated that 57 percent of the formerly unchurched and 54 percent of the transfer churched believed that relationships played a vital part in choosing a church.

2. W. Charles Arn, *How to Reach the Unchurched Families in Your Community* (Monrovia, CA: Church Growth Institute, n.d.).

3. George Barna, *Evangelism That Works* (Ventura, CA: Regal, 1995), 78.

4. Rainer, *Surprising Insights*, 43.

5. Joseph Aldrich, *Lifestyle Evangelism* (Portland, OR: Multnomah, 1981), 81–84.

6. Andy Stanley and Ed Young, *Can We Do That?* (West Monroe, LA: Howard, 2002), 1.

7. Paul Benjamin, *The Equipping Ministry* (Cincinnati: Standard, 1978).

Chapter 2: The Team Approach to Evangelism

1. John C. Maxwell and Tim Elmore, *The Power of Partnership in the Church* (Nashville: J Countryman, 1999), 9–10.

2. John Mark Terry, *Church Evangelism* (Nashville: Broadman & Holman, 1997), 90–92.

3. C. Gene Wilkes, *Jesus on Leadership* (Wheaton: Tyndale House, 1998).

Chapter 3: The Biblical Mandate for Evangelism

1. Tony Evans, *God's Glorious Church* (Chicago: Moody, 2003), 56, 59.

2. Aldrich, *Lifestyle Evangelism*, 102–3.

3. Rick Warren, *The Purpose Driven Church* (Grand Rapids: Zondervan, 1995), 32–33.

4. R. Kent Hughes, *Acts: The Church Afire* (Wheaton: Crossway, 1996), 48.

Chapter 4: The How-To of REACH Team Ministry, Part 1

1. Larry Gilbert, *Team Evangelism* (Lynchburg, VA: Church Growth Institute, 1991), 14.

2. The author highly recommends that you read Darrell W. Robinson's book, *Incredibly Gifted* (Garland, TX: Hannibal Books, 2002). Dr. Robinson details clearly and quite biblically that all the gifts of the Spirit are to be exercised through evangelistic efforts in order to fulfill the Great Commission and to bring people to a saving knowledge of Jesus Christ.

Chapter 5: The How-To of REACH Team Ministry, Part 2

1. Steve Sjogren, *Seeing beyond Church Walls* (Loveland, CO: Group, 2002), 16.

2. Ibid., 211–26. See also Steve Sjogren, *Conspiracy of Kindness: A Refreshing Approach to Sharing the Love of Jesus with Others* (Ventura, CA: Vine, 2003), which offers numerous ideas relating to random acts of kindness that can be demonstrated in the local community. For additional ideas, go to www.servant evangelism.com.

Chapter 6: The Role of the Pastor in Effective Leading and Training

1. Aldrich, *Lifestyle Evangelism*, 162.

2. Elton Trueblood, *The Company of the Committed* (New York: Harper & Row, 1962), 68–75.

3. Darrell W. Robinson, *Total Church Life* (Nashville: Broadman & Holman, 1985), 16–17.

4. Robert C. Anderson, *The Effective Pastor* (Chicago: Moody, 1985), 228–32. Anderson offers a variety of excuses and rationalizations that pastors and churches give to justify their lack of evangelism in the church.

5. Ibid., 231. Anderson points out that the gifts spoken about in Ephesians 4:11 are related to functional gifts, or positions given to the church as a division of labor and service. However, there is no indication relating to a specific gift of evangelism in the New Testament.

6. Lay Evangelism School, *WIN Teacher's Manual*, Baptist General Convention of Texas, Evangelism Division, n.d., 5.

7. Max Lucado, *The Applause of Heaven* (Dallas: Word, 1990), 20–21.

8. Robinson, *Total Church Life*, 146–49.

Chapter 7: New Beginnings to Some Old Endings

1. Author unknown.

2. Author unknown.

3. John MacArthur, *Hard to Believe* (Nashville: Thomas Nelson, 2003), 2.

4. Thom Rainer, *The Unchurched Next Door* (Grand Rapids: Zondervan, 2003), 24.

5. These figures are based upon research discovered in ibid.; Barna, *Evangelism That Works*; and statistics provided by the North American Mission Board of the Southern Baptist Convention.

6. Rainer, *Unchurched Next Door*, 25.

7. Ibid., 73.

8. John H. Yoder first developed these correlations in the article "Jesus Kind of Fisherman," in *Gospel Herald* (May 1, 1973): 375; see also Arthur G. McPhee, *Friendship Evangelism* (Grand Rapids: Zondervan, 1978), 44–48.

Chapter 9: The People Involved

1. William Fay, *Share Jesus without Fear* (Nashville: Broadman & Holman, 1999), 15.
2. Bill Bright, *Witnessing without Fear* (San Bernardino, CA: Here's Life, 1987), 67.

Chapter 10: The Process Involved

1. Barna, *Growing Your Church*, 91–92.
2. Ibid.
3. George Gallup Jr., *The People's Religion* (New York: Macmillan, 1989).
4. Elmer Towns, *An Inside Look at 10 of Today's Most Innovative Churches* (Ventura, CA: Regal, 1990), 235.
5. Rainer, *Surprising Insights*, 49.
6. Sjogren, *Conspiracy of Kindness*, 17. This book contains a detailed list of servant evangelism projects to consider. I highly recommend securing a copy.

Chapter 11: The Priority Involved

1. Randy Raysbrook, *One Verse Evangelism*, developed in conjunction with the Navigators and Dawson Press, Colorado Springs, copyright 2000. Used and adapted by permission of the copyright holder. To order the booklet, contact Dawson Media at www.dawsonmedia.com, or write Dawson Media, a ministry of the Navigators, P.O. Box 6000, Colorado Springs, CO 80934.
2. The "Handout" gospel presentation is used by permission of Dr. Kenneth Silva, Share Your Faith Ministries, Evangelism Explosion International; David Burton, director of evangelism for the Florida Baptist Convention; and John Rogers, director of evangelism for the state Convention of Baptists in Indiana. The "Handout" illustration used in this book is a combination of the above-mentioned authors' presentations.
3. Permission granted for use by the North American Mission Board of the Southern Baptist Convention, an agency supported by the Cooperative Program and the Annie Armstrong Easter Offering. For a copy of the booklet, contact NAMB, 4200 North Point Pkwy., Alpharetta, GA 30022-4176.

Chapter 12: The Power Involved

1. Kathleen Grant's book, *Advancing Christ's Kingdom: Praying in the Word of God*, teaches marvelous principles of praying for and seeking God's will through his Word. To attain a copy of this book, go online to www.prayerpartnerswithgod.com or call toll-free at (877) 267-2445.

Chapter 13: The Passion Involved

1. Michael Jordan, "For the Love of the Game: My Story," *World*, January 23, 1999, 9, 27.

2. Raymond McHenry, *McHenry's Stories for the Soul* (Peabody, MA: Hendrickson, 2001), 204–5.

3. William Morris, ed., *The American Heritage Dictionary of the English Language* (Boston: Houghton Mifflin, 1978), 958.

4. Spiros Zodhiates, ed., *The Hebrew-Greek Key Study Bible* (Grand Rapids: Baker, 1988), 1719.

5. Statistics published by the North American Mission Board of the Southern Baptist Convention in *New Churches Needed: A Step-by-Step Handbook for Planting New Churches* (Alpharetta, GA: North American Mission Board, 2001), vi.

6. *Webster's New Collegiate Dictionary* (Springfield, MA: G. & C. Merriam, 1981), 831.

7. K. Connie Kang, "Next Stop, the Pearly Gates . . . or Hell?" *Los Angeles Times*, October, 24, 2003, morning ed.

8. Thom Rainer, "Putting a Face on the Unchurched," *Church Planting and Evangelism Today*, North American Mission Board of the Southern Baptist Convention (fall 2003), 2.

9. George Barna, *Think Like Jesus* (Brentwood, TN: Integrity, 2003), 6.

10. David Barnett and Todd Johnson, *Our Globe and How to Reach It* (Birmingham: New Hope, 1990).

11. Maxwell and Elmore, *Power of Partnership*, 82.

Chapter 14: The Price Involved

1. Barna, *Evangelism That Works*, 24.

2. Adrian Rogers, interview by Ruben R. Raquel, February 2, 2002.

3. David Faust, *Taking the Truth Next Door* (Cincinnati: Standard, 1999), 24–28.

4. Andres Tapia, "Reaching the First Post-Christian Generation," *Christianity Today*, September 12, 1994, 19.

5. Fay, *Share Jesus without Fear*, 83–112. Bill Fay has compiled a list of thirty-six common objections that you might be subject to in a witnessing encounter. This is one of the most thorough lists available.

Chapter 15: The Payoff Involved

1. Fay, *Share Jesus without Fear*, 12.

2. Dan Reiland, "People Skills: Building Relationships That Work," *Joshua's Men* (Atlanta: Injoy Ministries, 1996).

3. Dale Carnegie, *How to Win Friends and Influence People*, rev. ed. (New York: Pocket Books, 1964), 92.

4. "On Average, We Watch 30 hours of T.V. a Week," *Chicago Tribune*, October 31, 1991, 6.

Epilogue

1. Margery Williams, *The Velveteen Rabbit* (New York: Avon, 1975), 16–18.

Scott G. Wilkins (M.Div., D.Min., Southwestern Baptist Theological Seminary) is a veteran pastor, having served over twenty-two years in churches in Texas, Georgia, Alabama, Indiana, and Kentucky. He presently serves as the lead pastor of the Master's Church, a new high-impact church plant in Lexington, Kentucky. He and his wife, Patty, have three children. This is his first book.

The REACH Network is the evangelism and high-impact church planting teaching ministry of Dr. Scott Wilkins. The burden of his heart is to teach every believer the importance of establishing evangelistic relationships and to encourage church leaders to consider planting new congregations. Dr. Wilkins travels extensively across North America and abroad teaching and training new Christians in evangelistic relationship-building principles and how to plant high impact churches.

Dr. Scott Wilkins is available for conferences, seminars, and speaking engagements. To contact him, please call, write, or email:

Dr. Scott Wilkins
The Master's Church
133 Trade Street, Suite 2
Lexington, KY 40511
(859) 246-3770
scottwilkins@alltel.net
www.reachnetwork.net